Ra

A Mitigator's Perspective

Adam C. Michels

ISBN: 978-1-09839-809-5

Dedication

This is book is dedicated to my family, radon clients, Northern Colorado realtors and all those working for positive environmental change.

Special dedication to my friend Don. Radon professional, business owner, loving husband and father.

Acknowledgment

Thank you to the radon and education community. The advancements over the past twenty years have been nothing short of amazing. Without the scientific community this book would never have been completed.

Thank you, also, to my wonderful editors for whipping this book into shape. Their help and resources have been an invaluable asset throughout this entire process.

And lastly, I thank you, the readers. Although this book is written to be a tool for the residential housing community, I hope it helps you examine the role of radon in your families' lives.

Table of Contents

Page Left Blank Intentionally

Chapter 1
Brief History of Radon

"In 1903, I finished my doctor's thesis and obtained the degree. At the end of the same year, the Nobel Prize was awarded jointly to Becquerel, my husband and me for the discovery of radioactivity and new radioactive elements."

-Marie Curie

The story of radon is intertwined with the history of modern chemistry. It was followed by one of the greatest discoveries of radioactivity by three honorable scientists whose work is admired to this date and used for future research.

Radon is recognized as one of the environmental pollutants which if humans are overexposed can cause illness and eventually cancer. Although it has been officially recognized since the beginning of last century, its effects on people have only recently been confirmed.

This book will give a unique perspective on the story of radon. We hope to provide readers with a background of some noble scientists and their contribution toward radioactivity, particularly radon and its development over the years. Studying radon will help us understand more about our environment and the complexities of this extremely rare chemical element.

The Erz Mountain Disease

Even though radon was identified in 1900, its effects were observed hundreds of years ago. German geologist and physician, Georgius Agricola (1494-1555), discovered a large number of lung diseases being diagnosed in the local miners. Another scientist, Paracelsus, a Swiss physician (1493-1541), examined the diseases among the local miners in the Mountains of

Eastern Europe and realized that most miners were dying from lung diseases resulting from dust and various gases present in the mines underground. Two physicians, Harting and Hesse, found in 1879 that the death rate of uranium miners in Germany and Czechoslovakia was reaching up to 75%. The German miners, who worked for more than ten years in the mines, were eventually diagnosed with the 'Erz Mountain' disease, which was later classified as lung cancer. Forty-two years later, in 1921, Margaret Uhlig suggested that the real cause of lung cancer could be radium emanations (radon).

In 1924, Ludwig and Lorenser proposed that the lung cancer of the local miners might be caused by radon gas present in the mines. The real reason for the increasing rate of lung cancer was discovered during 1924-1932 and proven by the evidence of radon gas and particles found in nearby areas and mines of Schoenberg, Germany, and Joachimstal, Czechoslovakia. Later, in 1932, Prichard and Sikl reasoned that most of the deaths from radium emanations occurred before the miners even reached the age of fifty.

The assumption that lung cancer among the miners was caused by radon gas was not confirmed until the research conducted by BEIR Report VI studied 60,000 miners from eight different countries, out of which 2,600 developed cancer and 700 showed symptoms of the disease.

Eleven major public health studies were conducted of underground miners exposed to radon. This was compared with new data on lung cancer in the general population. The research produced two models and depending on which one was used, radon contributed to either an estimated 15,400 or 21,800 of the approximately 157,400 lung cancer deaths every year in the US.

In the past ten years, research in Iowa, U.S.A. (which has a strong history of mining) showed that the frequency of death rate among women has significantly increased in residential areas due to extreme exposure to radon gas.

In 2005, the World Health Organization developed an international radon project to discover effective ways to curb the health influence of radon and raise public awareness about the consequences of radon exposure.

Radium, Radon, Radiation, Becquerel, and Curies

A German physicist, Wilhelm Roentgen, found in 1895 that he could develop a picture on a photographic plate without displaying the plate to the light. He sent an electric current through a sealed glass tube inside a black carton that contained gas at very low pressure. As a result, it created a picture of the bones in his wife's hands to appear on the plate. He had discovered X-rays. This discovery eventually earned him his first Nobel Prize in 1901 in the field of physics. French physicist, Henri Becquerel (1852-1908), heard about Roentgen's discovery of X-rays and took a jump on his research in 1896. Becquerel established that it was uranium ore spontaneously emitting invisible rays that developed the images on the plates. No electricity was mandatory in this experiment. This led to his discovery of radioactivity.

His work ignited Marie Curie and Pierre Curie, and as husband and wife, they worked together with Henri Becquerel on his findings of radioactivity. Marie Curie soon discovered that the element *thorium* emitted similar radiations. Most importantly, the strength of the radiation depended exclusively on the element's quantity and was not affected by physical or chemical variations. This led her to determine that radiation was coming from something essential within the atoms of each element. The idea was drastic and helped to refute the ancient model of atoms as undividable objects.

"One of our joys was to go into our workroom at night. We then perceived on all sides the feebly luminous silhouettes of the bottles or capsules. It was really a lovely sight and one always new to us. The glowing tubes looked like faint fairy lights." -Marie Curie

By focusing on a super-radioactive ore called pitchblende, the Curies recognized that uranium alone could not create all the radiation. So, were there other radioactive elements that might be accountable?

In 1898, they conveyed two new elements, *polonium*, named for Marie's native Poland, and *radium*, the Latin word for ray. They also devised the term radioactivity along the way. By 1902, they mined a tenth of a gram of pure radium chloride salt from numerous tons of pitchblende, an unbelievable breakthrough at that time. Later that year Pierre, Marie Curie, and Henri Becquerel shared the 1903 Nobel Prize in physics. The committee was originally not going to include Marie, but Pierre insisted his wife's contribution be recognized, making Marie Curie the first female laureate.

Radon was discovered in 1899 by Ernst Rutherford, Robert B. Owens and graduate student Harriet Brooks when observing radiations from thorium oxide. While conducting experiments in 1899 the Curies revealed that the air surrounding radium had started to turn radioactive. Their understanding made them believe that the radioactive energy emanated by radium caused this effect. In 1900 a German chemist, Friedrich Ernst Dorn (1848-1916) also reported radium compounds producing radioactive gas. He named this gas "radium emanation". In 1903 Andre-Louise Debierne observed similar radioactive gas from actinium.

Radon was finally isolated in 1909 by Sir Willian Ramsay and Robert Whytlaw-Gray, who revealed melting temperature and approximate density. The following year they also determined that it was the heaviest of the noble gases. In 1912, it was accepted by the International Commission for Atomic Weights. In 1923, the International Committee of Chemical Elements approved the terms *Radon*, *Thoron*, and *Actinon* to connect their relationships with the parent elements *Radium*, *Thorium*, and *Actinium*.

Radon Miracles

An Address

ON THE

NATURE AND PHYSIOLOGICAL ACTION
OF RADIUM EMANATIONS AND RAYS,

WITH OBSERVATIONS ON OTHER RAYS.

Delivered before the Royal Scottish Society of Arts.

By DAWSON TURNER, M.D.,

President of the Society ; Physician in Charge of the Electrical
Department, Edinburgh Royal Infirmary.

Radon led to numerous applications in physics and chemistry, but as with x-rays, the medical industry was still first to make the first use of it. In 1903, it was Pierre Curie and Henri Becquerel who jointly published the Nature and Physiological Action of Radium Emanations and Rays, which acted as a starting point for medical applications. On the initiative of Pierre Curie, the doctors at San Liu Hospital in Paris started to treat skin tumors by placing small radium needles in contact with the tumors. Very quickly, other doctors also learned to make use of radium radiation. People began flocking to the waiting rooms thrilled to be able to make small unsightly marks on their faces disappear with just a few applications of radium salt, also known as radium bromide.

A few hospitals equipped themselves with a radium bomb to treat deep tumors. Another technique was also developed, The Curie Theory, which consisted of inserting a platinum needle containing radium powder into a cancerous tumor. At first, the recovery rate was low but improved over the months. The medical journals are full of examples of radon proving to be a miracle cure. Hence, radon became the tool for fighting cancer - the disease that was thought to be incurable.

Marie Curie in a mobile X-ray vehicle c. 1917

"...radium could become very dangerous in criminal hands, and here the question can be raised whether mankind benefits from knowing the secrets of Nature, whether it is ready to profit from it or whether this knowledge will be harmful for it. The example of the discoveries of Nobel is characteristic, as powerful explosives have enabled man to do wonderful work. They are also terrible means of destruction of the hands of great criminals who are leading the peoples towards war. I am one of those who believe with Nobel that mankind will derive more good than harm from the new discoveries."

-Pierre Curie

The Roaring Twenties

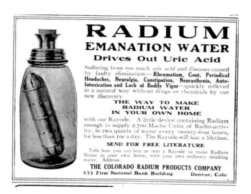

Praised for its benefits, radium became a magic potion, a panacea giving rise to flourishing businesses. Radium creams, tablets, toothpaste, and shampoos were believed to rejuvenate and cure chronic diseases such as rheumatism, arthritis, and gout. They were freely available in the open market. No authorization was needed as it was a natural product. The industry did not stop there. It used radium to make the hands and faces of watches and alarm clocks luminous. Manufacturers used it in tips of lightning conductors to improve their effectiveness.

Although the radium industry was expanding, the product remained extremely rare. Around 400 metric tons of ore had to be processed to extract a single gram of radium. No wonder it was 2,000 times more expensive than gold. One gram cost the same as a luxury house in Paris. It became so expensive that Marie Curie, who no longer had the means to buy it, could no longer obtain any. In 1921, a journalist organized a collection among American women in the United States. She collected $100,000, equivalent to well over a million dollars in today's money, to purchase a gram of radium for Marie. This gift was presented to her by the President of the United States of America. Only one and a half kilograms of radium was used worldwide before it was banned.

Evidence of the toxicity of radium was first collected in the United States of America in 1924. A New York dentist noticed an increasing number of cases of jaw cancer in his female patients. All had the same job, painting luminous numbers on the faces of alarm clocks, and were doing the same thing, dipping their paintbrushes in radium paint and putting them in their mouths to give them a fine point. However, the initial press articles reporting this news did not reflect public opinion.

The product was said to have so many virtues that people could not admit that there was a cause-and-effect relationship, especially since industries employing radium did their best to discredit those who questioned its safety. However, several commissions issued official alerts to American consumers when other suspicious deaths were reported including one young American, Evan Buyers. A wealthy industrialist, and ex-golf champion, died in 1931 from a radium overdose on the advice of his doctor. He had been systematically adding a product known as *Radithor* to his drinking water.

Incidents that occurred at factories like the Radium Luminous Materials in Newark show the real dangers of radium. Young women like fourteen-year-old Katherine Schaub used to pass their entire working day with tiny paintbrushes in their mouths and a small dish of radioactive radium powder sitting beside each girl. The radium powder mixed with a few drops of water and adhesive made a luminescent green paste called Undark, a mixture used to painstakingly paint numbers on the faces of watches. These girls were called dial painters, and they were instructed to hold the brushes in their mouths for increased precision. The illness that followed eventually led to a high-profile legal case, the first of its kind that paved the way to new developments in workers' laws.

Obviously, at that time, not enough research was conducted on the dangers of radium if it was, not much heed was paid by factory owners and managers regarding occupational health and safety. In her book, The Radium Girls: The Dark Story of America's Shining Women, Kate Moore tells the story of young women who were drawn to glamorous work with radium in the 1910s and 20s, only to have their lives taken— painfully, horrendously, and very early—by the lethal substance.

Protection Measure from Radium

The scandal in the United States that had affected the female clock painters marked a turning point in the history of radiation protection. At that time, protection was mainly concerned with external exposure for medical staff using screens-shielding and remote-handling devices. The painters in the U.S. factories were subjected to internal exposure as they ingested radioactive elements. The tragic fate of these women led to the establishment of a new type of standard - an ingestion limit.

The Decline of Radium

Radium's reputation, which had been so positive, was finally destroyed by the death of Marie Curie in 1934 from leukemia. Just a few months before her death, she had the pleasure of being present at the discovery of artificial radioactivity by her daughter and son-in-law.

Radium was gradually replaced by artificial radioactive elements such as cobalt, iridium, and cesium in medicine and tritium for luminous paints. It was finally prohibited in the 1970s as part of radiation protection regulations.

The Legacy of Radon

Although radon rays are no longer used today it has not gone away. Some industrial sites where it was used are still polluted by a residue that continues to emit radiation. One example is the Bayard clock factory, which flourished in the 1950s before finally closing in the late 1980s. The factory was then decontaminated. Every building and every square meter of the workshop was inspected. If radium was detected, the walls had to be scrapped, and the ground had to be dug up. After several years of decontamination work, 800 tons of waste was removed to the specialized storage centers run by the French National Agency for the management of radioactive waste. The waste only contained a few tenths of a gram of radium.

Many items containing radium were found in hospital cupboards, in the attics of doctors or their descendants, and even in the offices of solicitors and bankers who regarded radium as a financial investment. This is why campaigns were organized by IRSN, the French Nuclear Safety, and Radiation Protection Institute, to locate items containing radium and collect and store them in safe locations. In the campaigns in 1999, more than 500 items were collected.

The Curious Case of Stanley Watras

In 1984, construction engineer Stanley J. Watras was working at the Limerick Nuclear Power Plant in Pottstown, Pennsylvania. At the plant, monitors were installed to detect if workers accidentally contacted any unsafe dosage of radiation. One day at work, the radiation detector went off when Mr. Watras entered the plant. The safety personnel checked him thoroughly and could not find any source of radiation. Because the plant was under construction at that time no nuclear fuel was on site. Workers were also checked leaving for the day and so it was determined that the plant was not the source of the radiation.

Eventually, the workers discovered that Stanley was picking up the radon decay particles from home. A team of specialists investigated the case and found out that Mr. Stanley and his family were living in a home with levels ranging around 2700 picocuries per liter (pCi/L), more than 700 times higher than the EPA acceptable level. It was determined that the gas entered his house from underground.

If you want a glimpse of Madame Curie's belongings, including her cookbooks, manuscripts, clothes, or furniture, you have to sign a waiver and wear protective gear to shield yourself from radiation contamination. Her remains, too, were interred in a lead-lined coffin, keeping the radiation that was the heart of her research well contained.

Chapter 2
Radon and Geology

Now that we have covered a little bit about radon's history and its discovery, let's move on to discuss more about radon and geology. These topics are extremely complex, so here we will try to gloss over some of the basics while touching on a few areas that might not be so obvious.

Uranium

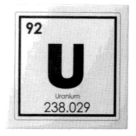

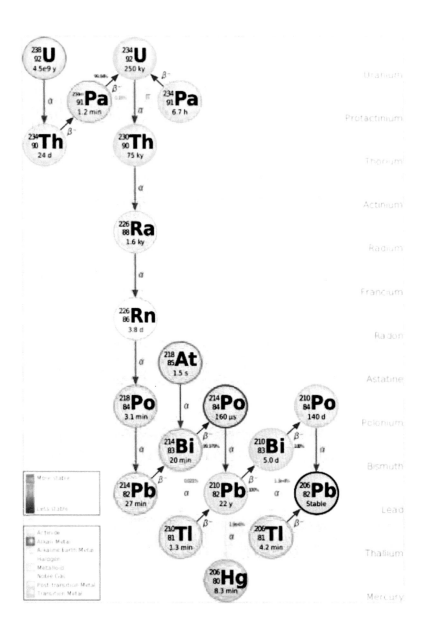

Uranium is a naturally occurring, weakly radioactive, silvery-greyish-white metal found in abundance in the earth's crust, discovered in 1789 by German chemist and pharmacist Martin Heinrich Klaproth. Most of the uranium we find in nature is Uranium 238 with a half-life of 4.5 billion years. All known isotopes of uranium are unstable. The element is not found alone but combined with others to make up a diverse collection of different minerals in soils around the world.

Uranium has been used as far back as medieval ancient Rome and the Middle Ages. Its orange-red to lemon-yellow shades of colors were used as coloring mediators in ceramic glazes and glass. Among the ordinary uses of uranium, it is widely employed by the military when making special weapons. It helps in the making of bullets and larger missiles hard enough to punch through armor. The most well know use of uranium would be its power and weapons capabilities.

Uranium ores of commercial-grade are commonly found around the world. On average, soils contain 2ppm of uranium minerals. Commercial value minerals contain several thousand parts per million of uranium oxides. Up to 40% of the world's uranium is mined in Kazakhstan. Other uranium mining countries include but are not limited to Canada, Australia, USA, South Africa, China, India, Romania, Ukraine, Brazil, and Russia.

Thorium

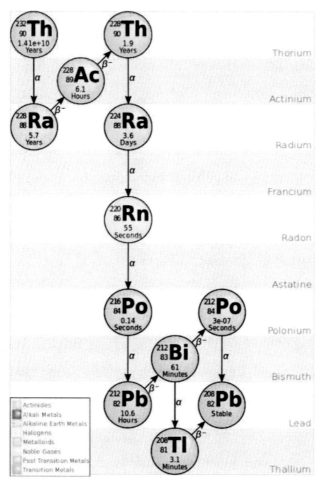

Thorium, named for Thor, the Norse God of thunder, was discovered in 1829 by Norwegian amateur geologist Morten Thrane Esmark and positively identified by Swedish chemist Jons Jacob Berzelius. The thorium series is led by thorium 232 which has a half-life of approximately 14 billion years, no stable isotopes, and is the parental element of radon-220 (thoron). The extremely long half-life makes thorium a tool in radioactive dating. While there are other thorium isotopes present in the decay chains, they only end up making very small portions of the total thorium available in the soil and rocks due to a shorter half-life. Thorium is about three times as plentiful as uranium in nature and the largest contributor to Earth's internal heat. There is perhaps more energy available from thorium than from both uranium and fossil fuels combined. China currently leads global research in this area, but original reactor designs come from work done at Oak Ridge National Laboratory, Tennessee, in the 1960s and early 1970s.

Thorium has had many uses in the past but has been substituted with other metals due to its radioactivity. An early commercial use would be inside street lights in the early 1900s. The thorium dioxide gas mantle created an attractive white light and soon became commonplace around Europe. Thorium is also used as a crucial alloying agent in magnesium, as it passes on greater strength and resistance at high temperatures. For this reason, it was used in ceramics and heat-resistant crucibles. The magnesium-thorium alloy is used in airplanes and space vehicles as well. Thorium was used to coat tungsten filaments in electronic tubes used in older television sets. Cathodes and anticathodes of X-ray tubes as well as the magnetron used in older microwave ovens all used filaments coated with thorium. It was previously added to glass, producing thoriated glass, during manufacture for use in high-quality camera lenses. Sometimes it was used in the making of jewelry. Thorium can also be used as a nuclear fuel in specially designed reactors.

In the earth's crust, thorium is found around 6ppm on average and occurs only as a minor part of many minerals. It is mined mainly in Brazil, India, Russia, and some parts of the United States. Large monzonite deposits found in some areas of the world can contain from 2% percent up to 20% thorium. Allanite, for example, may have 0.1-2% thorium as compared with zircon that might contain only 0.4% thorium.

Actinium

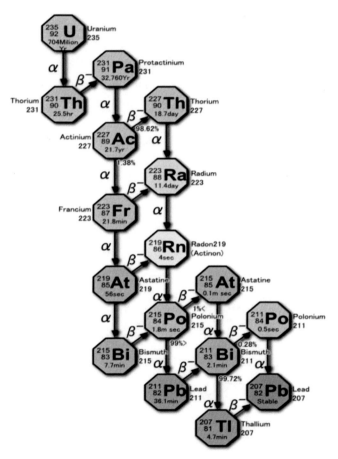

French chemist André-Louis Debierne claimed the discovery in 1899 while continuing research on the pitchblende residues from the Curie experiments. He was unable to isolate the new element but modern analysis revealed that he might actually been working with protactinium. In 1902, Friedrich Oskar Giesel successfully isolated the element, calling it "emamium".

Actinium is a silvery, highly radioactive, metal with similarities to that of lead. It is produced within the uranium 235 and thorium 232 decay series and has 32 radioactive isotopes. The actinium 227 isotope from uranium 235 has the longest half-life of approximately 21.7 years while actinium 228 from thorium 232 has a half life of 6.1 hours. Radon 219 (actinon) produced from the uranium 235 series is also extremely radioactive with a half-life of only four seconds. Due to its strong radioactivity, actinium produces a pale blue glow as its radioactivity ionizes the surrounding air. Actinium is found only in trace amounts in uranium ores. One ton of uranium ore might contain about 0.2 milligrams of actinium 227. Thorium ores might contain only about 5 nanograms of actinium 228 per ton of ore.

Actinium has very limited industrial application due to its radioactivity and cost. Research is being conducted on its viability for treating cancer and as possible source material in nuclear batteries for space travel.

Radium

Radium, discovered in 1898 by Pierre and Marie Curie is found mostly in uranium, and to a lesser extent thorium ores. Radium is an extremely difficult element to find in nature. Seven tons of ore might only yield about a gram of the element. Pure radium quickly reacts with the nitrogen in the air to form a black surface layer of radium nitride. Marie Curie and Andre-Louis Debierne isolated radium in its metallic state through electrolysis in 1911.

Radium is the heaviest known alkaline earth metal and highly radioactive. It is the only radioactive member of its group and parent to radon gas. The unstable nucleus will break down readily, producing ionizing radiation resulting in radioluminescence. Radium has thirty-three radioactive isotopes, most with extremely short half-lives. Radium 226 from uranium 238 has the longest half-life of 1600 years and produces radon 222 which accumulates in our homes. Radium 223 from uranium 235 has a half-life of 11.4 days. Radium 224 and 228 from the thorium decay series have half-lives of 3.6 days and 5.1 years.

Radon

Radon is a colorless, odorless, and tasteless noble gas. Most radon comes from decaying radium 226 and 224 in our environment. Radon gas has thirty-seven known isotopes. All are radioactive, but radon 222 is the most stable with a half-life of 3.8 days. As mentioned earlier, this is the radon that mostly builds up in the home.

The radon-220 isotope, which comes from thorium, has a half-life of only fifty-five seconds and is in much less abundant in nature. This short half-life provides less opportunity to accumulate and find an entry point into your home. Much of this radon and the other isotopes will break down in the soil matrix, but some very small amounts can enter your home if the sources are present and conditions are right.

Finally, radon 219 comes from actinium in the uranium 235 decay series. Radon 219 has a half-life of 3.9 seconds and is extremely rare in nature, as is uranium 235. Not much of a concern for homeowners, but it was included because it is another element that produces radon.

You are seeing traces left by Alpha particles produced by the decay of Radon 220 (half life 55 seconds) into Polonium 216.

As we look at the radon decay series there are a couple of details I would like to address. Radium is a solid, radon is a gas, and the radon daughters are also solids. Never again does it enter the gaseous phase after radon. The gas does not attract or attach to things. The solids do attract and attach to other particles.

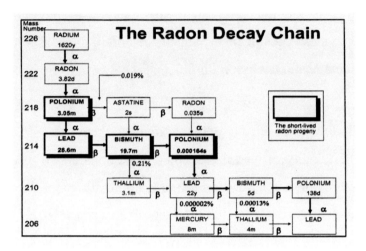

Here we have a Radon-222 decay cycle. As radon continues through the decay chain (radon daughters or radon progeny) polonium, lead, and bismuth are produced. The decay of the radon gas and the progeny they produce are the real problems.

Polonium is a rare and highly radioactive metal with no stable isotopes.   High energy = More damage!

Lead is a toxin that accumulates in soft tissues and bones. It acts as a neurotoxin, damaging the nervous system and interfering with the function of biological enzymes, causing neurological disorders such as brain damage and behavioral problems.

Bismuth has unusually low toxicity for heavy metals. As the toxicity of lead has become more apparent in recent years, there is increasing use of bismuth alloys (presently about a third of bismuth production) as a replacement for lead.

Of the three radon progeny, polonium is the "bad actor" of the group. Notice that all have very short half-lives with polonium having the shortest of the three. The topic of radon isotopes and the decay chains is extremely complex and well beyond the scope of this book. Wikipedia has excellent pages for reference on general information, decay chains, and isotopes of radon which cover those topics in much greater detail.

Minerals that contain Uranium and Thorium

Arsenates

Abernathyite
Kahlerite
Metazeunerite
Novacekite
Troegerite
Uranospathite
Uranospinite
Walpurgite

Carbonates

Andersonite
Bayleyite
Liebigite
Rabbittite
Rutherfordine
Schroeckingerite
Sharpite
Studtite
Swartzite
Voglite

Molybdates

Umohoite
Niobates-tantalates-
   titanates
Ampangabeite
Betafite
Brannerite
Calciosamarskite
Davidite
Delorenzite
Eschynite
Euxenite
Ferhusonite
Formanite
Irinite
Ishikawaite
Khlopinite

Microlite
Nohlite
Pisekite
Polycrase
Priocrase
Priorite
Pyrochlore
Samarskite

Oxides

Becquerelite
Billietite
Clarkeite
Curite
Epiianthinite
Fourmarierite
Ianthinite
Masuyite
Richetite
Schoepite
Thorianite
Uraninite
Uranosphaerite
Vandenbrandeite
Vandendriesscheite

Phosphates

Autunite
Bassetite
Cheralite
Dewindtite.
Dumontite
Frizscheite
Meta-autunite
Metatorbernite
Meta-uranocircite
Monazite
Parsonsite
Phosphuranylite
Renardite

Sabugalite
Saleeite
Torbernite
Uranospathite

Silicates

Beta-uranophane
Cheralite
Coffinite
Cuprosklodowskite
Gasunite
Huttonite
Kasolite
Pilbarlite
Sklodowskite
Soddyite
Thorite
Thorogrummite
Tscheffknite
Uranophane

Sulfates

Cuprozippeite
Johannite
Meta-Uranopilite
Schroeckingerite
Uranopilite
Zippeite

Vanadates

Carnotite
Ferghanite
Fritzscheite
Metatyuyamunite
Rauvite
Sengierite
Tyuyamunite
Uvanite

Source: Glossary of Uranium and Thorium-bearing minerals, 3rd Edition
1955, Judith Weiss Frondel, Michael Fleischer

Movement of Radon in Air

Since radon is a gas, it is more mobile than uranium, radium, and radon daughters which are found in the solid phase. Once radon has escaped the soil matrix and entered your home it moves about in strange ways being manipulated by gentle interior air currents. Each home is different and faces unique challenges. Here we look at some basic information on settling velocities and size to give us a better understanding of particle behavior. On the following page is a chart that shows how radon compares to particulates we encounter every day.

Large Particles- Larger than 100 μm (microns)

- Terminal velocity > 0.5m/s
- Fall out quickly
- Includes hail, snow, insect debris, room dust, soot aggregates, sand, gravel, and sea spray.

Medium Particles- in the range 1-100μm

- Sedimentation velocity greater than 0.2m/s
- Settles out slowly
- Includes fine crystals, pollen, hair, large bacteria, windblown dust, fly ash, coal dust, salt, fine sand, and small dust.

Small Particles- less than 1 μm

- Falls slowly, takes days to years to settle out of a quiet atmosphere. In a turbulent atmosphere, they may never settle out.
- Can be washed out by water or rain
- Includes viruses, small bacteria, metallurgical fumes, soot, oil smoke, tobacco smoke, clay, and fumes.

Folks sometimes ask... Is radon heavier than air? Why are radon levels higher in the basement than in the upper levels of the home?

The answer to the first question is...Yes. Radon is technically heavier than air, but at weights so small it does not matter. In most cases, it accumulates in the basement because it is closest to a source which would be in the soil under your home.

The human eye can usually see particles down to about 40 microns. Radon and oxygen are so small that it is easy to understand how they can move through pores and cracks in concrete right into our breathable airspace.

On the following page is a chart comparing radon with different types of particles. Look carefully at the size differences. Radon is much, much smaller than a micron and it takes days for particles of that size to settle out in a calm environment. Outside, the radioactive gas rides the air currents until it breaks down further or gets washed out by rain.

Particle	Particle Size μm (microns)
Gravel, very coarse (1.3 - 2.5 inches)	30000 - 65000
Gravel, coarse (0.6 - 1.3 inches)	15000 - 30000
Gravel, medium (0.3 inch)	8000
Gravel, fine (0.16 inch)	4000
Beach Sand	100 - 10000
Human Hair	17 - 181
Coffee	5 - 400
Dust Mites	100 - 300
Auto and Car Emission	1 - 150
Clay, medium	1 - 2
Household dust	0.05 - 100
Concrete pores	0.5 - 200
Atmospheric Dust	0.001 - 30
Radon Progeny Clusters Unattached	**0.0005 – 0.005**
Radon progeny Clusters Attached	**0.1 - 100**
Oxygen	**0.00015**
Radon	**0.00022**

* Size estimates for radon and oxygen were calculated using Van der Waals radius. Information for particle characteristics and sizes referenced from TheEngineeringToolbox.com. Progeny cluster estimates referenced from Activity of Ultrafine Fraction of Radon Progeny in Indoor Air.   Mohamed, Yuness, Abd El-Hady and Moustafa   Department of Physics, Faculty of Science, Minia University, Minia, Journal of Nuclear and Radiation Physics, Vol. 8, No. 1&2, pp. 65-78

Fun with Maps!!

Does one part of town have higher radon levels than another?

Even in residential developments with consistently high averages, some homes will still test low despite the results of the neighbors. Soil types and conditions can vary greatly within neighborhoods so it is extremely difficult to answer that question in detail. Included are four USGS maps that can give us a better look at uranium and thorium concentrations in the United States. The EPA radon map has also been included for reference. By looking at these maps together, we can begin to see patterns across the country and in your state.

There are two details about the maps that I would like to address. The first is that most of the United States has concentrations of radioactive material above one part per million (ppm) within the soil. Only roughly 10% of the country would qualify for having concentrations closer to zero, but even those areas are not void of radioactive material.

The second detail I would like to point out is the differences between the maps. The maps with the black background are dated 1993. The second set of uranium and thorium concentration maps was dated 2005. Technology improved quite a bit between 1993 and 2005 giving us more modern pictures. As we look at the images you can see all the variations in color within the same state and counties. These maps will continue to improve in time. It is important to remember that soil types can fluctuate greatly within a local area and at depth.

Testing for radon in homes is different than looking at soil mineral concentrations. The EPA radon map is still being developed and testing data is always being updated. Some areas simply have no recorded data. Variables such as home construction techniques, design, geographic location, topography, and interior use can all alter the radon data. I hope looking at all these maps together offers a new perspective for radioactive potential in the area where you live.

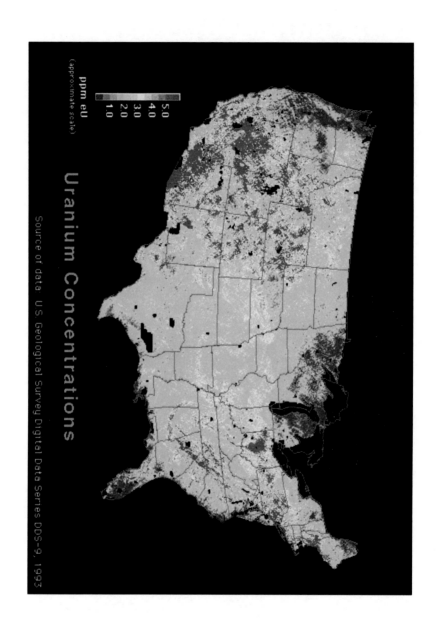

Uranium Concentrations

ppm eU
(approximate scale)

5.0
4.0
3.0
2.0
1.0

Source of data: U.S. Geological Survey Digital Data Series DDS-9, 1993

51

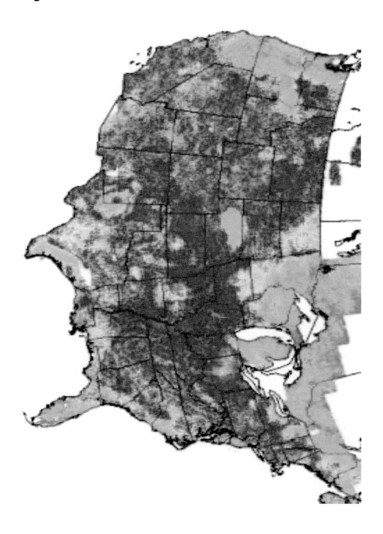

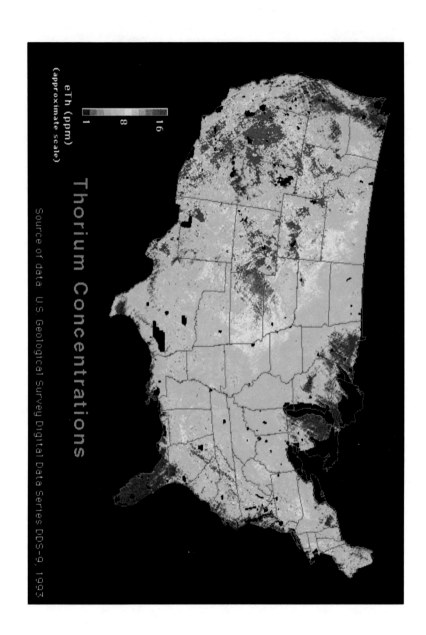

Thorium Concentrations

eTh (ppm)
(approximate scale)

1
8
16

Source of data: U.S. Geological Survey Digital Data Series DDS-9, 1993

53

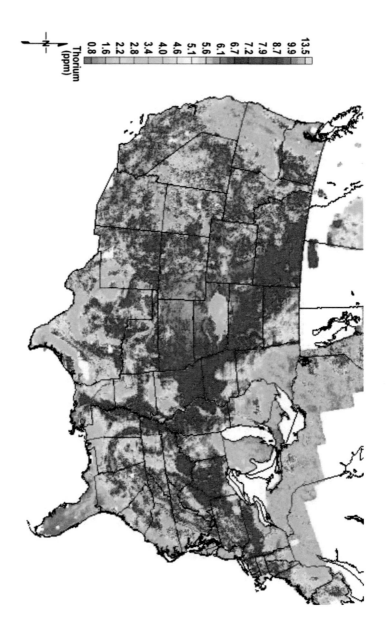

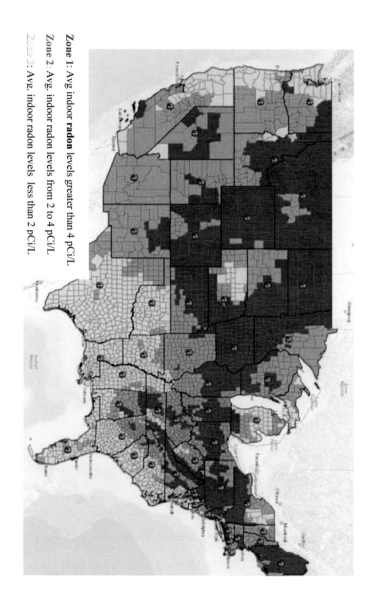

Zone 1: Avg indoor **radon** levels greater than 4 pCi/L

Zone 2: Avg. indoor radon levels from 2 to 4 pCi/L

Zone 3: Avg. indoor radon levels less than 2 pCi/L

55

Mineral Resources Data System

https://mrdata.usgs.gov/mrds/

Above is the link to the Mineral Resources Data System (MRDS). The MRDS is a collection of reports about mineral resources around the world. The page has two interactive areas to experiment with, commodity and record quality. The commodity area allows the user to single out different minerals and observe mine locations, past and present, across the world. The record quality sections separate the different reports by completeness, consistency, and quality of reference sources. Reports are graded A – E and you can plot the total amount of mining locations by grade.

The picture on the previous page is a copy of the commodity data for uranium from the MRDS. The different colored boxes and circles represent the different grade of that location. When you are on the website and zoom in closer to the land surface you notice the mine locations get farther and farther apart. Even though there are a lot of locations listed, there is plenty of area yet to explore. If you input uranium, thorium, and granite into the commodity map, you will see that it looks very similar to the radon maps.

RADIUM CONTAMINATION IN PUBLIC WATER SYSTEMS NATIONWIDE

https://www.ewg.org/interactive-maps/2018-radium/

The Environmental Working Group (EWG) has their own national tap water quality database comprised of data from approximately 50,000 community water systems across the USA. This specific map has data from

1850 community water systems serving populations over ten thousand and 1620 community water systems serving between three and ten thousand customers. Most of these systems use some sort of traditional filtration and disinfection before entering the distribution systems. Regardless, small amounts of radium can be detected after treatment. The significance of this map is to show radium in water is detected in most areas of the country. There are no private wells represented on the EWG map.

World Thorium and Uranium Reserves

Here we explore uranium and thorium reserve estimates from around the world. The numbers are only rough estimates, but my interest is the distribution. It is important to note that most countries do have some areas rich in both uranium and thorium deposits. -

Estimated Thorium Resources[1]

Country	Tonnes
India	846,000
Brazil	632,000
Australia	595,000
USA	595,000
Egypt	380,000
Turkey	374,000
Venezuela	300,000
Canada	172,000
Russia	155,000
South Africa	148,000
China	100,000
Norway	87,000
Greenland	86,000
Finland	60,000
Sweden	50,000
Kazakhstan	50,000
Other countries	1,725,000
World total	**6,355,000**

Source[1]: OECD NEA & IAEA, Uranium 2016: Resources, Production and Demand ('Red Book')

Uranium resources by country in 2019

	tonnes U	% of world
Australia	1,692,700	28%
Kazakhstan	906,800	15%
Canada	564,900	9%
Russia	486,000	8%
Namibia	448,300	7%
South Africa	320,900	5%
Brazil	276,800	5%
Niger	276,400	4%
China	248,900	4%
Mongolia	143,500	2%
Uzbekistan	132,300	2%
Ukraine	108,700	2%
Botswana	87,200	1%
Tanzania	58,200	1%
Jordan	52,500	1%
USA	47,900	1%
Other	295,800	5%
World total	**6,147,800**	

Source: OECD NEA & IAEA, *Uranium 2020: Resources, Production and Demand* ('Red Book')

Included below is some updated information on uranium supply from the World Nuclear Association website. According to the website, uranium resources increased by approximately 25% in the past decade simply due to increased mineral exploration. As identification techniques and technology improve, my guess is that this number will continue to increase. These statements also hold true for our radon maps. Increases in radon testing will continue to yield better, more

World Nuclear Association: Supply of Uranium

(Updated December 2018)

- Uranium is a relatively common metal, found in rocks and seawater. Economic concentrations of it are not uncommon.

- Quantities of mineral resources are greater than commonly perceived and are relative to both market prices and cost of extraction.

- The world's known uranium resources increased by at least one-quarter in the last decade due to increased mineral exploration.

Fracking

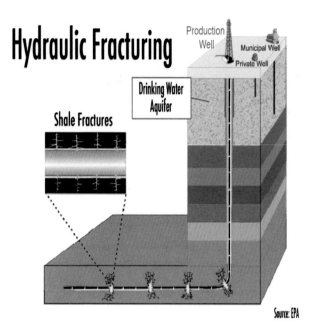

Hydraulic Fracturing

Production Well

Municipal Well

Private Well

Drinking Water Aquifer

Shale Fractures

Source: EPA

Fracking, also known as hydraulic fracturing, is a drilling technology used for the extraction of oil, natural gas, geothermal energy, and water from deep underground reserves. The process has been used in the United States since 1947. In fact, more than two million U.S. wells have been completed using this process, which can produce more than four billion barrels of crude oil and over twenty-eight trillion cubic feet of natural gas per year!

How Does the Process Work?

Simply put, fracking, or hydraulic fracturing, is carried out by injecting liquid and other materials at a high pressure to create small fractures within tight shale formations deep underground. The fractures stimulate the release and flow of resources where they can be pumped to the surface. Over 95% of today's wells use this technique. Companies frack older wells, which decreased in production or had been previously capped off, to expose new sources and bring them into profitability once again.

Fracking and Radon

A recent health study has discovered that hydraulic fracking of eccentric rock formation can accelerate the release of radon. Scientists at Johns Hopkins Bloomberg School of Public Health have established that radon level in the U.S. houses, particularly in Pennsylvania, has been increasing since fracking of the shale gas began in 2004.

The research was published in Environmental Health Perspectives and found that buildings constructed in areas abundant in shale gas mining had a comparatively higher level of radon than the buildings in low density and fracking activities. The research observed the radon levels in more than 700,000 buildings between 2004 and 2013. Buildings receiving water from ground supplies had 21% higher indoor radon levels than those being supplied from the municipal system.

The U.S. study of fracking results adds and supports previous studies by Australian researchers at Southern Cross University, including a recent shale gas study in

Colorado. It recommends that industrialized fracking can quicken the release of radon gas in geologies rich in uranium.

The topic of fracking is pretty popular in my area. Many of my customers live fairly close to active drilling sites. I have read a lot of local articles, professional papers, and attended seminars on the topic just to get an idea of how these activities affected radon. It is not hard to understand how complex these issues are and all the research needed to fully understand any impacts.

When looking at the EPA image, we can see how deep fracking is being performed. Fracking will release trapped radon underground which should exhaust at the wellhead creating elevated levels in these locations. My thoughts are that radon trapped under your homes should not change due to these activities but this seems to not be the case according to the study. Is fracking the main culprit here? Yes and no.

The average radon levels in your home are always fluctuating but the sources providing that radon remain constant long term. Here are my three main reasons for change in radon source material contributing to home indoor levels:

1. Additions to the structure.

2. Entrainment (physically bringing a radon source into the home).

3. Seismic activity, artificial or natural.

Energy waves moving through the soil matrix can shift strata, thus allowing previously trapped pockets of radon gas to more easily travel into your home. According to the USGS there are approximately 500,000 earthquakes worldwide each year. Out of that number, only 100,000 of those can be felt by us and only around 100 will do any kind of damage. Earthquake data does seem to run in cycles with some years releasing more energy than others. Currently, there are only 120 years of data with earlier numbers possibly being skewed.

Of the different scenarios leading to an increase in radon in your home, fracking is just one area of concern for some communities. The most important thing to remember is that higher mineral concentrations tend to be found in areas with larger oil and natural gas deposits. This generally results in higher radon averages for those surrounding residential communities.

Below is another table from the World Nuclear website that shows some examples of uranium concentrations in different areas and substrates.

Typical natural uranium concentrations

Very high-grade ore (Canada) – 20% U	200,000 ppm U
High-grade ore – 2% U	20,000 ppm U
Low-grade ore – 0.1% U	1000 ppm U
Very low-grade ore* (Namibia) – 0.01% U	100 ppm U
Granite	3-5 ppm U
Sedimentary rock	2-3 ppm U
Earth's continental crust (av)	2.8 ppm U
Seawater	0.003 ppm U

Thorium can be found in the soil at approximately 6 ppm.

Math Exercise!!

How deep would you have to dig to remove 1 million pounds of soil from under your home?

Average Home Footprint Size - 1000sq/ft.

Weight of Soil? 50-70lbs per cu/ft.

Uranium concentration – 2.8 ppm

Light Soil: 1000ft * (x) * 50lbs per cu/ft = 1,000,000lbs

50000x lbs. per cu/ft = 1,000,000lbs

x = 1,000,000lbs/50000lbs per cu/ft

X= 20 feet

Heavy Soil 1000ft * (x) * 70 lbs. per cu/ft = 1,000,000lbs

70000x lbs. per cu/ft = 1,000,000lbs

x = 1,000,000lbs/70000 lbs. per cu/ft

X = 14.28 feet

For this example, we would have to dig anywhere from fourteen to twenty feet to remove one million pounds of soil from under the home. For our efforts, we might come up with 2.8 pounds of radioactive minerals, more if you factor in the thorium. Not to worry. Most of this material will not be very radioactive but trace amounts very well could be. If you are interested in what mineral deposits look like in nature, YouTube has many different videos exploring old mines and areas of high radioactivity. These videos give a miners view of underground deposits and the lengths they had to go to extract the targeted ore. If you enjoy geology, these videos are a real treat.

Radon in Water

Radon can accumulate in the water. Water present in rivers and lakes has much less radon as compared to water available from deep wells. As the water flows through the soil matrix, radon, minerals, and contaminants enter drinking water sources. Alpha emitters such as radon are very plentiful under the earth's surface. When the water reaches an air-water interface, the radon will escape into the local atmosphere. In most instances the radon reaches the air outside and harmlessly floats away. Water pumped directly from wells, to point of use, can have high levels of radon at that location.

In most areas of the country, potable water supplied to homes comes from a surface water source and goes through a conventional treatment process. Some municipalities may use groundwater sources or a combination of both feeding into the water treatment plant. Conventional water treatment processes offer multiple opportunities for radon to escape into the atmosphere. Smaller municipalities and individual homeowners using groundwater sources might have a more closed system enabling radon to stay in the water until the point of use.

Many locations across the country are at risk of elevated levels of radon in groundwater. The EWG interactive map does not show radon but it does show that radium still makes its way into our potable water even when treated. This radium will produce small amounts of radon. Residential wells do not go to the depth of municipal or fracking wells but are still vulnerable to radon contamination. Local geology, groundwater flow, well recharge, and water extraction rates will all play a part in the amount of radon that comes from the tap. Check with your state and local groundwater offices for more information.

Radon and the Moon

Apollo 15 in 1971 passed 110 km above the Aristarchus plateau on the Moon and discovered a considerable rise in alpha particles thought to be caused by the decay of Rn-222. The occurrence of radon was confirmed later from data obtained from the Lunar Prospector alpha particle spectrometer. Other elements that are known to exist on the moon include thorium, oxygen, magnesium, manganese, silicon, calcium, titanium, and iron.

Data from the recent moon landing of Chinese space probe Chang'e-4 showed very high radiation levels on the lunar surface. The recorded levels were about 10% higher than the radium/thorium-rich beach sands in Brazil which can reach over 500 times normal background exposure.

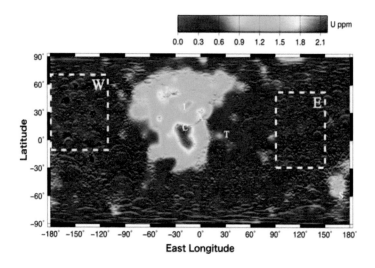

A map of uranium levels on the lunar surface, as measured by the Kaguya mission. The highest levels are at 2.1 parts per million (ppm) at Copernicus crater (C). E and W stand for the east and west highlands on the far side of the moon; A, the Apennine Bench; I, Mare Imbrium; J, Montes Jura; S, South Pole — Aitken Terrane; and T, Mare Tranquillitatis.

(Image credit: N. Yamashita et al., Geophysical Research Letters)

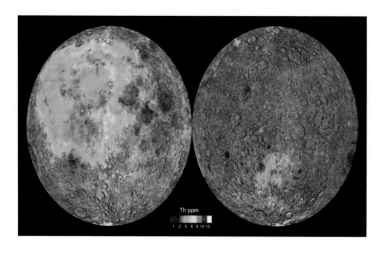

Image: Data: NASA / ARC / Jeff Gillis; map by Paul Spudis

The gravity of the moon influences the tides here on earth. This same moon gravity also influences the movement of radon. As we have mentioned before, radon is a gas. Water is a liquid. Both gas and liquid are considered fluids. When the moon moves the water, it moves the radon too. How much influence does the moon have on radon? Water is much denser than radon and we witness tidal change every day. My guess is that moon gravity can have a significant effect on indoor radon levels if conditions are right.

Chapter 3
Radon Testing

The United States is one of many countries where residents may face high levels of radon gas in their homes. Current estimates are about 1 out of every 15 homes in the US has elevated radon levels with some areas observing much higher ratios. Since radon is a colorless and odorless gas, the only way we can know the levels in any structure is through testing.

The Environmental Protection Agency (EPA) suggests that every house in the United States should be tested for radon. Previously, most people were of the view that homes without a basement were not at risk, but this is not the case.

Testing for radon can be is easy and inexpensive for the proactive homeowner. Indoor and outdoor environmental conditions constantly change and thus create fluctuation in daily radon levels. This chapter will look at testing basics, different types of radon testing kits, radon testing devices, radon units, radon entry points, and what can happen when conditions change.

Radon Testing Basics

Radon gas is being created in the soil underneath our homes and is moving up through the soil matrix. Different areas underneath our homes contain different levels of radon. Some areas can be very low and some areas can be very high. When looking at radon measurements underneath a concrete basement floor, we notice how different the levels can be from one area to another.

Here is an example of how levels can fluctuate underneath the basement floor:

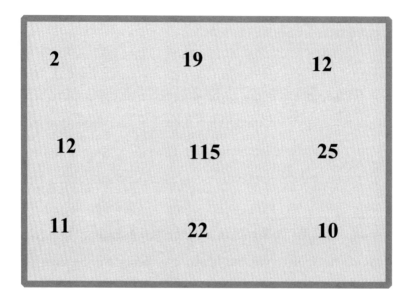

In this example, the indoor levels might only be 8-10pCi/L on average, but when conditions change, there is a reserve of gas ready to enter the home.

EPA Action Limit = 4.0pCi/L

As the radon builds up under the basement, it slowly infiltrates into the lower level of the home through cracks in the concrete, sump systems, foundation gaps, crawlspaces, utility lines, and even through the concrete itself. As the daily weather and seasons change, radon levels in the home also change.

Radon testing can be performed in many locations around the house, but it is best to follow the EPA recommendations for testing. Here are the basic rules when testing your home for radon:

- Radon tests should be performed on the lowest, livable area within the home.
- EPA recommends placing radon test kits in the general living space or bedrooms of the lowest level.
- The test kits should be kept away from heaters, vents, and indoor fans.
- Testing devices should not be placed in bathrooms, storage closets, around kitchen areas, or in crawlspaces.

- Test kits should be placed at least 3 feet from any exterior window or door, at least 20 inches off the ground, and a minimum of 12 inches away from indoor walls.

One misconception is that a house that is closed for a prolonged period will test higher due to inactivity. This assumption is false. Most homes have windows and doors closed for the majority of the year. Normal exit and entry do not introduce enough fresh air to significantly change radon levels. Radon is also constantly breaking down. If there were no new input of gas, the levels would simply drop to roughly zero.

Types of Radon Tests

Whether you've had your house tested for radon or not, it is beneficial to understand the two most common types of radon testing, active and passive. These types of tests can be done short or long term. A short-term test would last from two to seven days, where a long-term test might last from thirty days to a year. Next, we will quickly look at a few examples of both active and passive test devices. Remember that there are many different types of testing equipment on the market. Be sure that tests are conducted using approved EPA methods and techniques.

Active Testing

Professional active testing is done using some type of continuous radon monitor (CRM). The CRM measures and records the level of radon in the air on an hourly basis for as long as the meter is deployed. Many of these units will also measure temperature, humidity, and alpha counts plus give error codes if there is a loss of power or the unit has been moved. The monitors require a yearly calibration to help ensure the accuracy of the data. Test results can also be downloaded to compatible software for detailed customer reports. The advantage of active testing is that the homeowner can see how the radon fluctuated throughout the test.

Rad Star Continuous Radon Monitor

The Rad Star CRM uses a pulse mode ionization chamber for analyzing radon activity. Each unit has different features depending on the model. Yearly calibration is required and the data is downloadable.

Sun Nuclear Continuous Radon Monitor

Here is a picture of Sun Nuclear Model 1028 Professional Continuous Radon Monitor. This model uses a diffused-junction photodiode sensor to measure the concentration of radon gas. Similar to the previous example as data can be downloaded and yearly calibration is recommended.

Safety Siren Pro Series 3 Radon Gas Detector

The Safety Siren Pro Series 3 Radon Gas Detector is an example of a common home unit for sale on the internet and in retail locations. This model uses an ionization chamber to help calculate radon levels. This unit displays long and short term averages, not individual hourly readings. If you would like to see if the detector is working properly, you will have to do another test alongside the unit to confirm the measurements. This is a good idea with any household radon detector. As with any mass-produced product, consumers have reported instances where the unit displayed extreme and/or incorrect values. Conducting a side-by-side test with a short-term passive kit, or other radon measurement device will help confirm the detector is working within acceptable limits.

Passive Testing

Passive radon testing does not require electricity to function. It is carried out by placing single or multiple test devices inside the home for a specific length of time, then the device is sent to a laboratory for analysis. This type of testing gives an overall average of the radon level in that area during deployment. Many different types of passive radon testing kits are available today. Both short-term and long-term devices are inexpensive and easy to use. Below are a few examples of current passive testing kits available on the market and a brief explanation of how they work.

- Activated Charcoal Absorption (short term): Here are two examples of activated charcoal test kits. Radon and daughters adsorb onto the charcoal and then are measured at a lab using a sodium iodide counter. The kit on the left is a pouch that is usually hung from the ceiling during the test duration. The kit on the right is a picture of a canister test device. Simply open and place the canister in an acceptable testing location. Close and seal canister at test completion and send to the lab for analysis.

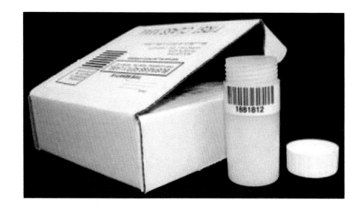

- Charcoal Liquid Scintillation (short term): This device is similar to the previous test kits in that the radon and daughters adsorb onto the charcoal. Any present radioactive particles are converted into light using a liquid scintillation medium, and then counted in a scintillation detector.

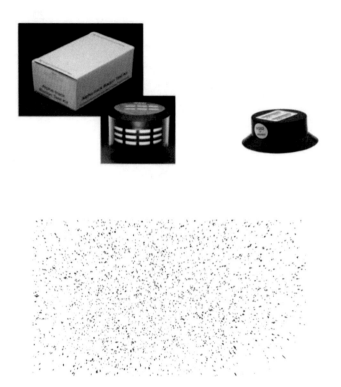

- Alpha Track (long or short term): The alpha track detectors have a special foil inside the device. Alpha particles from decaying radon create tracks on the foil upon impact. During analysis, the foil is chemically treated to enlarge the tracks so they may be counted and a radon level determined.

- E-Perm / Electret Ion Chamber (short or long term): The Electret Ion Chamber contains a positively charged Teflon disk inside a small chamber of electrically conducting plastic. Negative ions inside the device get collected on the electrate and reduce the charge. The reduction in charge is measured, and this data is used to calculate a radon level for the duration of the test.

Radon Units and Radioactivity

The measurement of radon and its decay products is expressed in several ways. It is important to get a basic understanding of what these units mean. The level of radon in the air is measured in units of Becquerel per cubic meter (Bq/m^3) in most parts of the world. In the United States, we use picocuries per liter (pCi/L).

One Becquerel (Bq/m^3) is defined as the amount of nucleus decay per second per square meter of air.

A picocurie per liter (pCi/l) is defined as the level of radon gas in one liter of air in which 2.2 atoms of radon decay per minute.

TABLE III. Units of Measurement of Radioactivity and Dose

Quantity	Unit	Purpose	Comments
Activity	Becquerel (Bq)	Measure activity of a radioactive material (solid or gas); the International System of Units (SI) definition of activity	I Bq = I atomic disintegration per second
	Curie	In the United States, the activity (rate of decay) of ^{226}Rn is expressed in units called curies	The curie is based on the rate of decay of one gram of ^{226}Ra or 3.7×10^{10} disintegrations per second
	Pico curies (pCi)		I pCi = one trillionth of a curie; 0.037 disintegrations per second, or 2.22 disintegrations per minute
Radioactivity in air or water	Becquerels/m^3 (Bq m^{-3})	Measure average concentration of radon gas in building or in soil air Bq/L used to measure radon in water	Average level of radon in houses in Great Britain is 20 Bq m^{-3}; in Sweden 108 Bq m^{-3}
	pico curies/L (pCi L^{-1})	Unit used in the United States	Average level of radon in houses in the United States is 1.24 pCi L^{-1} equivalent to 46 Bq m^{-3}
Absorbed dose	Gray (Gy)	Measure energy per unit mass absorbed by tissue	I joule of energy absorbed by I kg of tissue
	rad	Old unit of absorbed dose	I rad = 0.01 Gy
Dose equivalent	Sievert (Sv)	Measure of absorbed doses caused by different types of radiation	Absorbed dose weighted for harmfulness of different radiations
	Roentgen equivalent man (rem)	Old measure of absorbed dose	The rem is being replaced by the Sievert, which is equal to 100 rem

The table above shows some of the ways radioactivity and dose are measured and what the measurements mean.

Now let's take a quick look at some indoor/outdoor averages and frequent radon unit conversions.

The conversion from becquerels to picocuries is roughly:

$$1 \text{ Bq/m}^3 = 37 \text{ pCi/L}$$

Standard indoor exposures average about

0.03 Bq/m^3 or 1.24 pCi/L.

Standard outdoor exposures average about

0.01 Bq/m^3 or 0.4 pCi/L.

In the mining industry, the exposure of radon is generally measured in Working Levels (WL) and the collective exposure in Working Level Months (WLM).

One **working level** is roughly the concentration of radon decay products per liter of air in equilibrium with 2.7 Bq/m ^{3} or 100 pCi/L of radon gas. The WLM would simply be the accumulation of exposure over 170 hours, roughly equating to a 40-hour workweek.

Radioactivity

The topic of radioactivity is extremely complex. Let's quickly review two important areas that I feel are most important for folks to understand, Inverse Square Law and Half-life.

Inverse Square Law:

Intensity is inversely proportional to the square of the distance of the source.

THE INVERSE SQUARE RULE

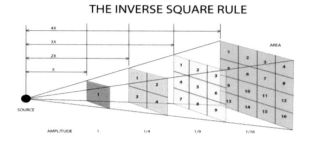

* https://docsaleeby.blogspot.com/2016/12/electromagnetic-radiation-and.html

$$Intensity = 1/d^2$$

Radon gas gets into the lungs and decays. The close distance makes the intensity greater!

Half-life: the time required for a quantity to be half of its initial value.

Starting Concentration = 12pCi/l

Radon 222 half-life = 3.8 days

New concentration after: 3.8 days = 6pCi/l*

7.6 days = 3pCi/l*

11.4 days = 1.5pCi/l*

* providing no new additional radon enters the testing area

Important Radioactivity Rule:

The longer the half-life, the **more** stable the nuclide.

The shorter the half-life, the **less** stable the nuclide.

Less stable nuclides are more active, create more radiation, more daughters, and therefore are more dangerous to us. Radon is less stable and has a short half-life.

Radon Testing in Water

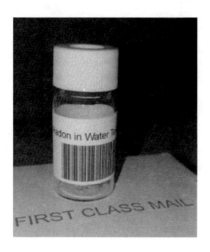

Currently, there is no EPA-mandated MCL for radon. If your water source is from a personal well, then the homeowner is responsible for understanding water quality and treatment options. Average residential well depth in the U.S.A. ranges from 100 to 200 feet. The maps in chapter 2 show that most of the country has some amount of radioactivity in the soil. The water quality reports do not have an MCL for radon, but there is one for radium. Reductions in radium will result in reductions of radon in the water.

Indoor residential radon water to air conversion:

10,000pCi/L (water) = 1pCi/L (air)

Radon in water MCL if equivalent to outdoor air levels:

4000pCi/L (water) = 0.4pCi/L (air)

EPA Proposed MCL for Radon:

300pCi/L for Water

MCL for Radium:

5pCi/L for Water

It takes a lot of radon in the water to raise home indoor air levels significantly. Even the EPA proposed MCL for radon seems like a lot to consume. Radon in water can reach levels well over 100,000pCi/L in many areas of the country so it is something to take seriously. Test kits purchased online can vary in price depending on the lab and services performed. The EPA has a drinking water hotline available for homeowners with more information about state offices, certified laboratories, and other relevant information. Included below are links to Kansas State University, North Carolina Department of Health and Human Services websites for radon in water, and the State of Maine website for well water testing. These sites are an excellent reference for homeowners and explain in more detail the specifics of radon in water. EPA encourages all homeowners with private wells to test for radon.

Safe Drinking Water Hotline (1-800-426-4791)

https://sosradon.org/water-testing

http://www.ncradon.org/Radionuclides.html

https://www.maine.gov/dhhs/mecdc/environmental-health/eohp/wells/mewellwater.htm

Stories from the Field

For this section, I would like to take the opportunity to share some of my personal experiences with radon at home and in the field. Some of them were quite astonishing. Later, we will revisit the significance of these stories.

My Radon Story

In December 2004, I was handed the key to my first new home. Being a new home, the basement was completely unfinished, and I had visions of one day finishing it. I knew the first thing I needed to do was test the radon level. I pulled out a passive test kit from my supply and set it up in the basement. Sure enough, it tested high at 12 pCi/l. Within a few days of receiving my test results, my helper and I installed a new radon system. As we were finishing up, I did some airflow tests underneath the basement slab. Happy with the airflow results, I never retested the basement.

About two years later, I received some work that required more detailed testing than the simple passive test kits would provide. I ordered a continuous radon monitor from a radon supply company expecting to keep the monitor for only a few months and then return it once the project was completed. When the monitor arrived, it was a very professional-looking unit, complete with a tripod, carrying case, and printer. Since I had no experience with the unit, I decided to use it on my home and see if I could replicate the results that I obtained with my passive test kit years ago. Luckily, it was close to the same time of year as the first test, so I turned off my mitigation system, set up the monitor, turned it on, and closed the basement door.

A few days later, I remembered the monitor was in the basement and headed downstairs. We had a few more days before the monitor was needed, so I decided to do a little experiment. I opened the basement windows for about five minutes, closed them back up, turned on my mitigation system, and rushed upstairs to answer my ringing phone. My basement has four large windows and was unfinished at the time, which allowed a nice breeze to flow through. The monitor was untouched for another day or so before I finally returned to see what had happened. I never looked at the data on the machine. I just followed my instruction manual and printed out the results. This is what I found:

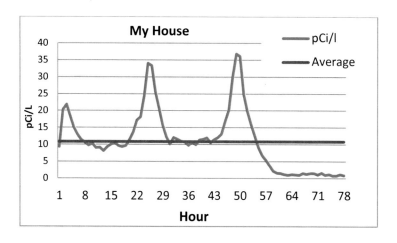

I was shocked at what I saw. My home's radon average had not changed. The average was still about 12 pCi/l like the passive test showed, but my home had climbed to the 30pCi/l range twice during the testing period. My system did a good job of dropping the levels, but the fluctuation was disturbing. I had seen almost a 200% increase from the passive kit results and my system had been running only moments before the test was started.

Story 2: Gusty Winds

I was mitigating a new home for a client at a location close to one of our local rivers. The homeowner was in the process of moving in, and there was nothing in the basement. The basement was around 1200 sq/ft in size, about average for that area and it was very windy that day, maybe 25-40 mph gusts. After setting up, I started working on the floor penetration in the basement. The floor penetration went in easily, and it seemed fairly hollow underneath the basement slab. The sub-slab material was comprised of large gravel (some over three inches in diameter) and very loose, sandy dirt. Quite unusual for my area but maybe not so unusual for this housing development being so close to the river.

As I reached under the slab to remove some material, there was a strong gust of wind. Just as the wind blew, you could feel the air from under the basement floor blow right in my face. I was a little startled by what had happened, but sure enough, another strong gust came through, and it happened again with a bit more velocity. This was the first time I could noticeably feel the movement of sub-slab air and how strong it was. Even though the wind was gusting that day, it was extremely impressive how much force was being exerted on the air underneath the basement floor that day.

Story 3: Flood Storm

This home was first tested by the previous homeowner using a passive test kit yielding an initial radon reading of about 9 pCi/l. The homeowner was not satisfied with the passive test result, so his realtor recommended that I come in with a radon meter and try to verify the homeowner's results. During the retest, we had a storm that produced local flooding and heavy winds. These are the results of my retest of his home. The house was vacant at this time.

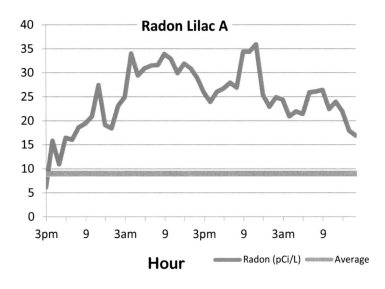

After observing the retest results, it was decided to mitigate the home. I offered the homeowner a discount if I could use his home as a test subject. To my surprise, he agreed. My idea was to start the meter a day or so before the test, let the meter run during the installation and then for 48 hours after completion. The windows were opened during the installation, and then closed before we left for the day. The mitigation system installation went well with no issues and the meter was left in the home. We returned 48 hours later and printed out our results.

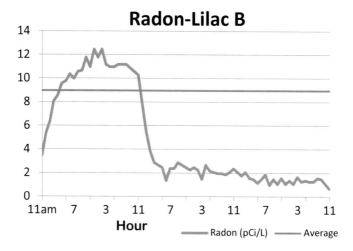

The pre-mitigation numbers are very close to the 9 pCi/L that the homeowner obtained with his passive test kit. We also see that the mitigation system slowly decreases the radon level in the room until we start to level out around 1 pCi/L after 24 hours.

Super Spike

This last chart was given to me by a customer after her home was tested by another company. We were both shocked at how high the level had reached. There were periods of very high winds (+35mph) during the test which were not uncommon for the area. The house was a nicely designed 2500sq/ft home in a master-planned community, built about 2007 with a basement around 1200sq/ft. Another interesting detail about this test was how the levels dropped after the weather system passed. The post-peak average (grey line) was about 25% lower than the pre-peak average (orange line) with levels trending downward. Based on this example, a similar home with similar characteristics and a weaker radon source could only be testing 5-7pCi/L on average during pleasant conditions but then jump into the 13-30pCi/L range during poor weather conditions.

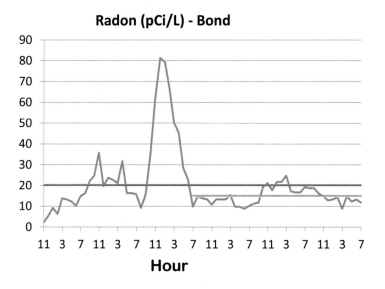

Radon (pCi/L) - Bond

Lost Data

Many years back I did a radon test for a customer's rental unit. The unit was under contract and the home had never been tested. It was mid-July and very nice weather. The radon meter was placed in the lowest level of the home adjacent to a medium-sized crawlspace and left for 48 hours. When I returned the results were printed out and eventually given to the homeowner. No other copies were made and the data was lost. I asked the tenant if anything had happened that night. He said he opened his bedroom window around 3 am to cool the room down. Opening the window in the upstairs bedroom caused a spike in radon in the room with the radon meter. Unfortunately, the room being tested was his children's bedroom.

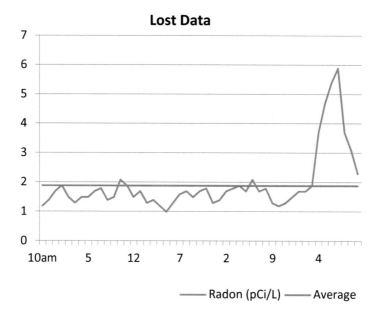

Lost Data

Radon (pCi/L) ——— Average

The examples have been selected because they show how much radon can fluctuate indoors. Flood Storm, Super Spike, and the Gusty Wind stories all occurred during very high winds. My Radon Story and Lost Data happened during much milder weather conditions yet we still see dramatic increases when indoor conditions change. There are several influences that can affect radon levels, but here let's look specifically at the wind.

How often do wind conditions increase to speeds that might cause a significant increase in radon levels?

To answer this question, I pulled up some historical data on wind speed from the Weather Underground website. The data used is from February and July 2016. These months were selected because they were the most extreme. In my area, February is generally the coldest month of the year, and July the hottest.

Normal daily wind speeds generally range from 5-12mph depending on location. Here let's focus on wind speeds over 20mph normally representing gusty conditions. Ironically, both months had roughly six to eight days where wind gusts were of significant speeds. This would equate to 25-30% of the time or equal to 91 to 110 days per year the home is possibly under gusty conditions.

Gusty conditions can help contribute to extreme radon

increases. The rate at which radon enters the home is completely site-specific but is heavily influenced by the wind velocity. These charts help put into perspective the opportunity that exists for radon levels to spike for a normal month. Most months follow these same types of trends all year long.

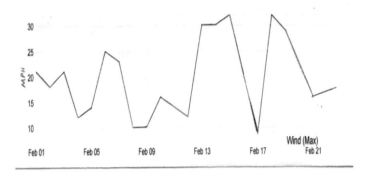

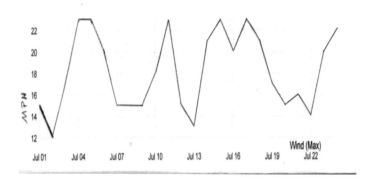

Testing for radon is an easy yet tricky process that can be influenced by a lot of factors. The examples in this chapter are extreme but not unusual. Short-term testing, active or passive, can completely miss fluctuations due to the short testing period. Long-term testing can miss these fluctuations also because many long-term tests are done passively. If you do a long-term active test, then fluctuations in the radon levels will be displayed or recorded by the testing device. Radon is so small that it moves and acts in ways we are not accustomed to. Be sure to test your home under different weather conditions to get a better understanding of radon level changes.

Radon Influences:
- Internal: Exhaust fans, heat sources, opening windows, radon in water, home additions, emanation
- External: Wind, barometric pressure, precipitation, seasons, soil types, groundwater movement, tectonic activity
- Celestial: Sun, moon, other

Chapter 4
Radon Mitigation

The basic principles of radon mitigation are fairly simple, but the application of installing a system can be labor intensive and confusing. This section looks at the basics of radon mitigation and how to prep your home for a successful mitigation system.

Basic System Types for Radon Mitigation

Active Systems: An active system uses the suction of an inline fan to draw the gas from beneath the home, through the system and exhaust it outside. Most of these systems also include a manometer to show airflow.

Passive Systems: Passive radon systems are piping configurations designed for sub-slab gas removal. When properly installed, these systems work with normal internal and external forces to help move the gas from beneath the home to the exterior and away from the breathable airspace. No electricity or fan is involved.

System Categories

Most homes I have encountered fall into one of three categories;

- Full basement
- Full crawlspace
- Partial basement and crawlspace.

These descriptions relate to the footprint of the home and are the areas that need to be addressed. The footprint would refer to any part of the home that is touching or directly over the ground surface.

Sub Slab Depression System (SSD): Exterior

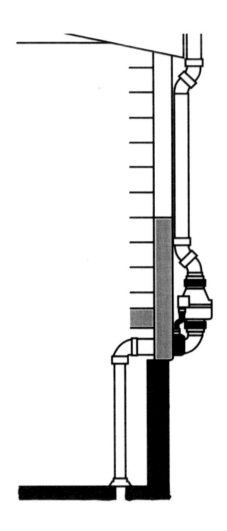

Sub Slab Depression System (SSD): Interior

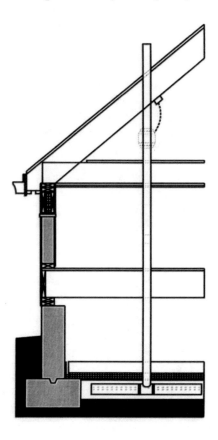

Sub-Membrane Depressurization System (SMD)

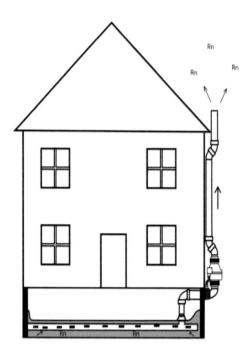

Combination Sub-Slab/Membrane Depressurization System (Combo).

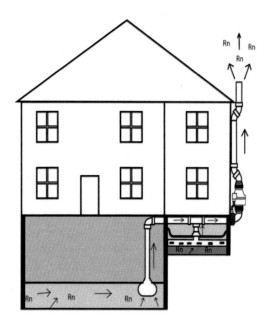

All three systems work on the same basic principles: trap the radon gas, create an area of negative pressure and then exhaust the soil gas to the exterior. Let's examine a basic SSD system and how it works.

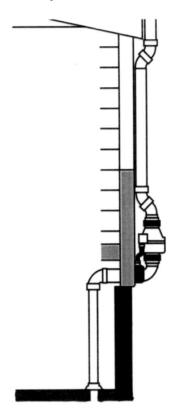

Here is an excellent example of an exterior sub-slab depressurization system. These systems are constructed by creating about a 4.5-inch diameter penetration through the basement floor and removing 5-10 gallons of soil from underneath the concrete slab called a suction pit. The suction pit helps open up pathways under the concrete for soil gas to flow into the system. Next, a four-inch pipe is inserted into the floor penetration, routed up the foundation wall, through the rim joist, and to the outside of the home. The fan is mounted on the exterior and vented up to discharge above the roofline. A system manometer is installed on the interior pipe in a visible and accessible location inside the home.

Radon System Manometer

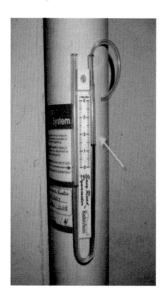

Above is a picture of a simple U tube manometer commonly used with radon systems. The manometer has two basic functions.

1. It lets you know that the fan is on or off. When the fluid levels are uneven, as in the picture, the fan is running. This is how we want the manometer to look. When the levels are even, the fan is not running.

2. The numbers in the middle of the manometer refer to inches of water. Each fan has an airflow chart so the technician can see how much air is being moved from under the slab based on these numbers. The higher the number, the less air movement. A well designed system with piping under the concrete slab, manometer numbers should be around 0.5 or less. Homes with more resistance to air flow and no piping under the slab will have higher numbers.

When the radon system is turned on the fan creates an area of low pressure under the floor. This area of low pressure attracts soil gas, moisture, and radon. A properly installed radon system can easily move air under a large basement floor when pipe and a permeable material is present. This same system type also works well with slab-on-grade structures.

If your home doesn't have a basement, but a crawlspace, then an SMD system is the type to be installed. Inside the crawlspace, a perforated pipe is installed upon the soil surface under the barrier. The objective is to install the pipe in a configuration that will provide any buildup of soil gas a relatively short path to the system pipe. Finally, the perimeter seams and areas around supporting structures are all sealed. When the fan is turned on, air currents are created underneath the vapor barrier exhausting the contaminated air outside.

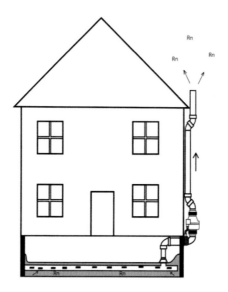

The final type of radon mitigation system I would like to highlight is a combination system.

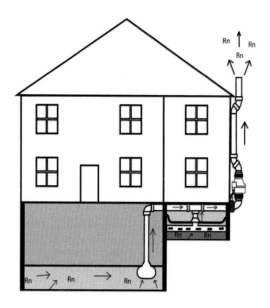

This system type would be used when the home has a lower-level basement along with an adjacent crawlspace. In the illustration, the pipe has been routed into the crawlspace and then continued to a floor penetration located in the home's basement slab. The pipe in the crawlspace is smaller and lightly perforated so that the system will collect the gas accumulating under the barrier in the crawlspace while still maintaining adequate airflow at the suction pit. These systems can be designed in a few different ways to incorporate multiple areas. Larger homes may need multiple systems or high-capacity fans to do the job. Each home is unique and requires a specific plan.

Getting ready for an installation

So you found out you have a radon problem and have scheduled an installation. What now? Preparation for an installation of a radon mitigation system is pretty straightforward but can be time-consuming if the basement is full of homeowner's items. For simplicity's sake, let's assume the basement is completely unfinished with no crawlspaces.

First, identify the installation location. Provide a clear workspace for personnel and equipment at the floor penetration location and any other areas in question.

Second, move any items away from exterior perimeter walls and off of floor expansion joints. Identify the sump pit, bathroom rough-ins, and any pipe penetrations through the concrete floor. Allow access to those areas for inspection.

Third, vacuum debris from wall perimeter and expansion joints paying close attention to corners, under stairs, and behind drain pipes. Excessive debris will keep caulking from sticking to concrete and providing a good seal.

Finally, it is good to remember that the technician needs to provide power to the radon fan. This means running a wire from a hot power source to the radon fan on/off switch then finally to the fan itself. Many basements only have one electrical outlet available often located around the stairs or furnace. Keep the areas around power outlets accessible. It is also important to identify which breaker on the electrical panel will shut the power off to the radon system. This breaker should be clearly labeled after installation to avoid confusion in the future.

Crawlspace

Many times the crawlspace underneath a home gets neglected. It can serve as a storage area for many different bizarre items or a home for various types of critters. Close inspection is the best way to get a clear understanding of any activity happening in these areas. Crawlspaces should be inspected every couple of years for rodent or insect activity. The ideal crawlspace for mitigation is easy to enter, relatively flat, clear of storage items, debris, pests, and cobwebs with some kind of adequate lighting. If you are going to use your crawlspace for storage after installing a radon system, try to acquire some old carpet remnants or cardboard boxes to provide additional protection for your radon barrier. Activity on top of the radon barrier can create separation and punctures in high-traffic areas. Be especially careful in crawlspaces with uneven slopes, excessive rocks, debris, sharp concrete, and other unique features. Mitigation systems help create a better crawlspace work environment for any repair, upgrades, or additions that may be done in the future.

After twenty years of experience, I am a firm believer that all homes with crawlspaces should have active SMD systems. Whether your reason is dust suppression, moisture, critter problems, or radon, SMD systems make a huge difference in the air within the crawlspace environment and in your home.

Attics

Many times radon systems are routed through the attic of a home or garage. If you feel your home might be a good candidate for one of these systems being proactive can ease the installation process, especially in older homes.

First, start by inspecting the attic area keeping safety in mind. Old storage items or other obstacles can exist that homeowners are unaware of. Remove and dispose of any items that are easily accessible. If larger items exist in the space take some pictures and formulate a plan for removal if they are an obstacle to the installation.

Second, try to identify an attic light or source of power for a radon fan. This is not always easy to identify. Most newer garage attics have a hot power source or light already installed. Power can also be obtained from garage door opener outlets in the garage ceiling if other options are not available. If you know of a usable power source, try identifying the corresponding electrical breaker. Many times a power source is not obvious. This is also good information to know before installation.

Passive Systems

An effective passive system can be created for any type of home with any type of footprint. Passive systems work best when designed for a specific home and installed during construction. The more complex the footprint, the more difficult it is to get higher levels of removal efficiency. A well-designed passive system can obtain removal rates of 50% and higher! A poorly designed system can have removal rates of 0% efficiency and provide the homeowner with additional expense if radon mitigation is needed for that home. Chapter 7 has an in-depth look at the passive system design and configuration. Always refer to a trained and experienced professional when designing any passive radon system. The number of incorrectly installed passive radon systems is simply staggering.

Venting the System

There are different methods for venting a radon system in Canada and the United States. In Canada, radon fans can be mounted indoors and vented close to ground level. Codes in the USA require radon systems to be vented at least ten feet above grade and preferably above the roofline. Customers have concerns about the ability of the radon to re-enter the home or accumulate in an area adjacent to the system. To better understand what is going on, let's look at radon exhaust and discuss a little bit about particle dynamics as mentioned in chapter two.

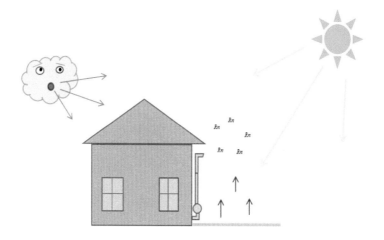

Here we have an illustration of a normal home with a radon system on the exterior. On sunny days the radiation warms the ground creating heat currents that move upward. The wind is usually blowing with speeds ranging around 5mph on a calm day and 15mph, or more, on a gusty day.

The highest concentration of contaminants will be located within twelve inches of your exhaust vent. As the air moves away from the exhaust location it quickly dilutes with the outside air. If you were to take samples at a location eight feet directly in front of your exhaust, with no wind, you might get some residual readings. If the wind is moving at any velocity you might not be able to catch any radon or daughters in your sample.

In Chapter 2 we looked at sedimentation rates and particle sizes. The radon and radon daughters are super small and act in ways unique to its size. The gas does not like to attach and will get whisked away from a combination of heat currents and wind. Radon daughters are solids and do like to attach to heavier objects. The particle clusters may be large compared to the daughters themselves but they are still too small to settle and accumulate. The farther the air moves from the exhaust, the more it mixes and dilutes down to undetectable levels.

The YouTube program, Veritasium, featuring Derek Muller, released an episode called, Turbulent Flow is MORE Awesome Than Laminar Flow. Here the host and friend explain their arguments as to which type of flow is better or more appealing. Air from our radon systems is probably in turbulent flow well before it exhausts outside. The exterior air is in turbulent flow as well. Check out the video if you want to learn more about the crazy complexities of turbulent flow.

Mobile / Manufactured Homes

Any structure on the ground surface has the potential for radon accumulation. Mobile and manufactured homes do not sit directly on the ground but can still accumulate radon. A lot of it has to do with how the home is skirted. Many homes have plastic skirting with vent holes built in. The vents allow the gas to move out from under the unit and not accumulate in most cases. If the skirting has no type of venting or limited venting, then soil gas can accumulate. Vapor barriers alone will not stop soil gas from reaching the home. Units with stronger source material underneath may require the assistance of an active mitigation system even with skirt venting. The larger the footprint of the structure the greater the probability of radon accumulation underneath and inside the home. Testing is always a good idea.

Air Purifiers and Plants

Many times, a little radon still enters the home even with an effective running system. Radon gas and the radon daughter clusters are too small to be filtered out on their own. If the daughters cluster and attach to indoor dust particles, residential air purifiers can be effective. Dust sources are both internal and external, so there is a constant supply.

HVAC home filters can be effective in removing particulates, but they require the system to be running to clean the air. The cleanliness of the ducts themselves must also be considered. Individual room air purifiers can provide more of a consistent, efficient filtration directly at your location. There are many different models and designs to choose from which offer varying levels of filtration. A properly maintained purifier can remove airborne dust which will promote better sleep and health.

In April 2016, the University of Alabama's nursing and engineering departments, supported by NASA's Advanced Exploration Systems (AES) Life Support Systems Project, conducted a study looking at VOC removal by plants in an International Space Station environment. The focus plant was the Golden Pothos houseplant. The results show a reduction in VOC contaminants with the introduction of the plants. If the plants can reduce some VOCs in the air, they may also be able to take in radon gas or daughters, thus decreasing concentrations in that general area. Below is the link to the Golden Pothos study along with links to a couple of other articles that look at a few different plant species and air contaminant removal.

https://ntrs.nasa.gov/archive/nasa/casi.ntrs.nasa.gov/201

60005687.pdf

https://www.livescience.com/38445-indoor-plants-clean-

air.html

https://www.ecowatch.com/20-plants-that-improve-air-

quality-in-your-home-1938383954.html

Radon Mitigation in Well Water

Once issues with water quality have been identified with your source, then you can begin to look at treatment options. The two most common ways to remove radon are aeration and granulated activated carbon filtration (GAC).

Aeration units involve injecting air through water or water through air depending on the design. This helps the radon move from the water and into the air where it is exhausted outside. The installation of this type of unit is a bit more involved and costly, but it does come with a few advantages. Aeration units provide excellent radon and VOC removal plus it exhausts the radon outside so it does not continue decaying in the unit. These systems may require a bit more maintenance than filtration but can remove higher levels of radon. Maintenance for the units will vary based on the manufacturer and design.

Radon Airation Unit

Granulated activated carbon filtration is another radon removal method. Radon, uranium, radium, and the daughters can get trapped in the filter where it breaks down further. The filters are exchanged on a regular schedule to avoid excessive contaminate buildup. When radon can no longer be trapped inside the filter radon moves right through to the tap. This method might be used if low levels have been conformed through testing.

All the variables should be considered when selecting a filter for your home. Different types of technology do exist in the marketplace. It is always best to work with experienced professionals when designing and installing these systems.

Treating radon in water can be a sizable investment but it is still small in comparison to health care bills. It is hard to imagine enjoying a bath or shower, knowing that you are breathing excessive amounts of radon with every drop of water coming from your tap. Do not be fooled, radon may not be the only gas creeping into your water supply! If you look closely at our map section, you will see that all states have areas of high radioactivity. Many areas of the United States have significant underground natural gas reserves as shown in Figure 16. Smaller pockets of natural gas or other contaminants can exist locally but are never represented on any map. Testing is the only way to know if radon or other contaminants are an issue at your location.

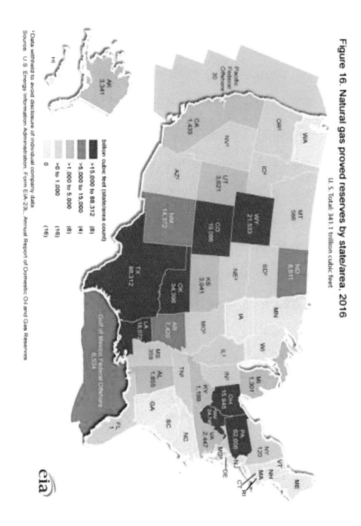

Figure 16. Natural gas proved reserves by state/area, 2016
U.S. Total: 341.1 trillion cubic feet

billion cubic feet (state/area count)

>15,000 to 88,312	(8)
>5,000 to 15,000	(4)
>1,000 to 5,000	(8)
>0 to 1,000	(16)
0	(16)

AK 3,341

Pacific Federal Offshore 30

CA 1,433

NV²

OR²

WA

AZ²

UT 3,621

ID²

MT 596

WY 21,533

CO 19,096

NM 14,372

ND 8,611

SD²

NE²

KS 3,041

OK 34,366

TX 88,312

LA 18,072

AR 7,420

Gulf of Mexico Federal Offshore 6,554

MO²

MS 359

AL 1,986

TN²

KY 1,199

IA

MN

WI

IL²

IN²

MI 1,301

OH 15,945

WV 24²

PA 62,656

VA 2,487

NY 120

GA

SC

NC

FL 1

MD²

NJ²

DE

CT RI

MA

NH

VT

ME

HI

eia

¹ Data withheld to avoid disclosure of individual company data.
Source: U.S. Energy Information Administration, Form EIA-23L, Annual Report of Domestic Oil and Gas Reserves

142

Chapter 5
Realtor Section

During my time in the radon business, I have seen the economy speed up and slow down. Changes in the market create changes in industry standards, mortgage practices, and the needs of the customer. With all the details involved in a real estate transaction, radon testing and mitigation often were overlooked or ignored due to fear of losing a prospective buyer. This section is dedicated to helping realtors assist their clients in getting through the "radon" process with as little turbulence as possible.

Each person needs to be dealt with differently and is in a unique stage in their lives. Sometimes the sale of a home can mean a new opportunity or addition to the family. Other times it may mean a family separation, tragedy, or the loss of employment. Either way, it is good to prepare your seller for the possibility of radon mitigation. I like to use the *"broken furnace"* example when discussing radon with homeowners. Someone can sell your home with the furnace broken, but most people will request it be repaired before closing.

Over the years mortgage companies have been requesting radon testing data and mitigation before approving a residential home loan. Sellers need to understand that buyers are becoming more aware of radon. Installing a well-designed mitigation system not only adds value to the home but might provide confidence to a prospective buyer that the current owners are concerned about indoor air quality.

With most real estate transactions, once an acceptable property has been found a potential buyer calls an inspection company to check the home over. This is usually the time when a radon test is performed. If the radon is found to be above the acceptable range, then the seller needs to make the decision whether to correct the problem, get an estimate, and credit the new homeowners, or just negotiate possible adjustments on the final purchase price. The difficulty with this whole process is that the home inspection and radon test are often done after the prospective buyer has agreed they like the property and are seriously interested in buying.

At this stage of the sale, folks may be in a hurry providing extra stress to the sellers and more money out of pocket as radon might not be the only issue that needs correcting. Sellers placed in this position of having to install a radon mitigation system last minute may be upset about this expense, accept the lowest possible bid and have a system installed which isn't aesthetically pleasing or installed correctly. This may lead to an unhappy customer, possible additional costs for the new homeowners, or worse an increase in radon levels. The more knowledge the realtor has, the better they will be at correctly navigating their customers through the entire process.

Radon Testing Options

Once a realtor has discussed the issue of radon with a seller, they may decide to be proactive before a new family is ready to buy. As we have reviewed in earlier chapters, radon testing can be done in one of two ways, active or passive. Homeowners may want to call on a professional radon tester or home inspector to conduct the test. Testing through a professional will usually cost around $200.00 and take about forty-eight hours to complete. Homeowners do have the option of conducting a passive test themselves at less cost. Passive radon testing can be done under $30.00 but involves a little effort and planning on the part of the homeowner. It is very important that if a homeowner is going to conduct a test themselves that they closely follow proper testing procedure. Conducting multiple tests at the same time is also recommended. Sellers need to understand that even if a mitigation system has been installed, buyers will most likely have the inspector conduct another test to verify results.

Realtors can aid in this process in several ways.

- Have a list of qualified radon professionals and a range of prices for services in your area. Prices for testing are far more consistent than for mitigation systems. The more complicated the installation, the higher the price in most cases. Try to stay away from a set number. Best to provide a price range for services in your area. Discuss price ranges with professionals in your local area before relaying information to customers.

- Know where to purchase radon test kits, and the approximate time it takes to conduct these tests. (Municipalities, Lowes, Home Depot, radon websites, etc.)

- Have this book or other reference materials available for customers.

Calling for Estimates

The house tested above the 4.0pCi /L action level, and it is time to obtain some estimates for fixing the problem. Generally, it is a good idea to obtain two to three estimates so clients can compare prices, warranty, and system design. Many radon contractors require a physical inspection before committing to a price for a mitigation system. In some cases, when the estimator is familiar with a particular builder or home design, they will give estimates over the phone. Before we start calling around and setting up estimates, let's gather a few pieces of important information about the property to help aid this process.

- **Full property address** - Pay special attention to east, west, north, south designators and correct zip codes. Be sure to include the correct home number and street name whether it is a street, court, way, or avenue.

- **Year house was built and renovation dates (if any).** Building techniques and codes change over the years. Knowing whether the house was built in 2010 or 1910 is always important. If the home has been renovated, try to identify what year that work was done and the scale of the project. The more information about the home history the better.

- **Basement size and layout**- The MLS listing should have accurate data for the size of the basement but not necessarily the home footprint. If the lower level seems to be a bit smaller than the level above it, inquire about a hidden crawlspace if none is mentioned. Crawlspaces are often used in new homes, in older homes, and under renovations. When the basement is unfinished, it is easier to locate smaller crawlspaces. Discuss these issues with the homeowner if things are unclear so the home's entire footprint is accounted for.

- **Radon levels** – What are the radon levels for the home and how was that data obtained? Test duration, location, and weather conditions are also important details to help radon personnel make better mitigation decisions.

- **Passive System** - Is there a passive system installed by the builder? Was the basement and sump pit sealed? Is there a labeled pipe for radon? Many newer homes have passive systems installed by the builder but they make not be easy to identify.

At first, this seems like a lot, but we can condense this down to five simple pieces of information:

1. Address   2. Year   3. Size   4. Levels   5. Passive

Providing this detailed information can help radon estimators get a better understanding of the property before showing up for an estimate. It can also help mitigation companies give more accurate phone estimates when the installation is going to be less complicated. Some companies may or may not ask for this specific information. Either way, having this information on hand before calling for estimates can save time and effort instead of searching for home information while on the phone or at a remote location.

Pipe Identification

Identifying all the different pipes within a home can be confusing even to us professionals. Radon pipes look very similar to drainage pipes used for the rest of the home. Let's take a look at the most common pipes found in the basement and how to differentiate a waste pipe from a pipe designated for radon removal.

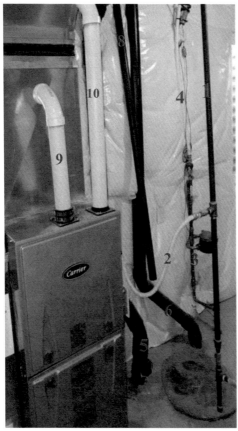

1. Rigid gas line
2. Flexible gas line
3. Potable water line copper and usage meter
4. Pex potable water line
5. Greywater drain pipe
6. Radon pipe
7. Sump pit
8. Sump pump drain pipe
9. Furnace air intake
10. Furnace

1. White Pex pipe cold water

2. Red Pex pipe hot water

3. Gas line main

4. Drain pipe

5. HVAC return duct from furnace

6

7

6. Water main line and meter (copper)
7. Sump pit with lid

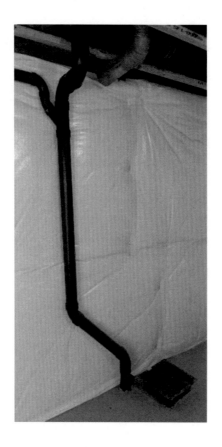

Wastewater drain pipe with connecting
smaller pipe at the top, access at the base for
cleanout if needed. Concrete cut out for
tub/shower drain in floor.

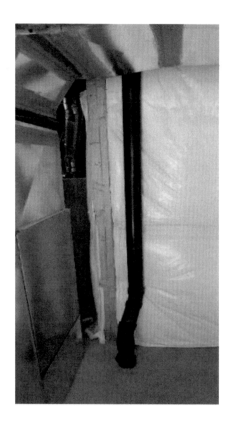

Wastewater drain pipe with access at base. Sink connections may exist but hard to see with the placement of HVAC ducts. Looks a lot like a radon pipe.

Here is a radon pipe. Same diameter as waste-water pipe but no access at the base.

Radon and sump pit drain pipes routed through the upper level. Radon pipes will not connect with any other pipes other than possible crawlspace extension. The pipe continues up to attic space and through the roof. Waste pipe will extend to the side of the home where water is discharged.

In this picture, we are looking at the same utility area just from a slightly different angle. The picture on the left is the primary direction from which a person would look at these utilities. The concrete residue helps to create an illusion that the front pipe is the pipe going into the concrete or that the pipes are connected. The picture on the right shows the passive radon pipe behind the water heater going into the concrete. The smaller pipe is just a discharge for the sump pit. These pipes are not labeled so it is important to inspect these areas carefully when determining if a passive radon pipe was installed.

There are many holes, gaps, and separations through the concrete to let in radon. A portion of the homes sewer and potable water pipes lead from outside of the home's foot-print to the interior space possibly contributing to more radon into the home. Lets look at some common entry points that should be addressed especially before finishing an area.

Here is a picture of the concrete cut-out for the drain under your basement tub. These holes usually range about one foot wide and two feet deep. It is very important to have these holes sealed with foam during bathroom construction. The cut-out can greatly decrease the efficiency of a passive or active radon system and can let soil gas into the home.

Above is an unsealed basement corner. Corners and areas behind pipes see the most dramatic separation. If not sealed when a system is activated, these areas will leak air and make a whistling sound if close enough to the suction point.

1. Passive radon pipe close to a wall. Separation occurred allowing gas, insect, and rodent entry. Possible back drafting issues if activated.

2. 2" grey water drain close to unfinished perimeter wall in the basement. Separation behind pipe and along wall/floor intersection.

Foundation Gaps

Foundation gaps - Unfortunately backfilling will not
seal these areas completely. Moisture and critters
always seem to find a way inside.

Here is an example of water entry into a crawlspace. You can see the three-quarter-inch gravel under the footer and the dark color of the moist soils. Water has found its way inside and created pathways.

This picture is a good example of a soil gas entry point next to a water line entering the home. Both sewer and water lines extend from the home to the main stem many feet away creating a conduit for soil gas to flow.

Soil types, mineral content, and porosity can quickly change in the local area of your home.

Finished Basements

When it comes to finished basements and radon mitigation, the installation will either be straightforward or difficult and frustrating. Realtors can usually walk into a finished basement and know whether the work was done by an experienced individual or someone with lesser experience and not as qualified.

Sometimes customers will make the mistake of saying a basement is unfinished when framing has already been installed. A finished basement would be defined as a basement with framing, electrical, plumbing, drywall, trim work, flooring, texture, and paint. Sometimes older homes have paneling instead of drywall. Whatever the case may be, if an area does not meet these criteria, the basement should be described as partly finished.

Photos in chapter 5 are from unfinished basements, some with insulation wrap on the walls. This allows for the perimeter wall-slab joint to be sealed as well as areas behind pipes to be addressed. Once framing has begun these areas become inaccessible and can allow radon entry. Understanding the difference between unfinished, partly finished, and fully finished will help add clarity, especially if trying to give an estimate without walking the property.

In cases where the basement is finished, realtors can be proactive by simply noticing where the unfinished areas are located. Are they in the front or rear of the home? Is the unfinished space centrally located or to the side of the basement against an exterior wall? Is the room with the furnace and water heater finished? Do they even have any unfinished space? Is there a sump pit or any other openings in the concrete? Was anything sealed? Is there a crawlspace? If so, does it have a vapor barrier? Does the vapor barrier cover the soil surface? Has the barrier been sealed to a wall?

Keeping these questions in mind will help prepare for radon-related issues. Another extremely helpful tool is the camera app on our phones. Photoshoots of homes rarely contain pictures of unfinished spaces and utility rooms. Take a few pictures from different angles and perspectives of every room in the home including the exterior. Many realtors are including a 3-D option for customer viewing of homes for sale. I have found this option incredibly helpful when doing estimates without an in-person visit. Unfortunately, the 3-D viewing does not always show behind every obstacle and this is where additional pictures can be helpful. Radon professionals are always grateful to know as many of these little details as possible in preparing for estimates.

System Placement Basics

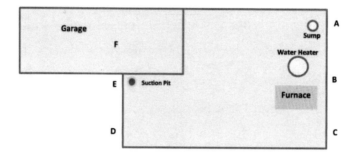

Here we are going to look at some installation options A - F for an active radon mitigation system. Radon systems can be installed hundreds of ways, but here we will focus on six typical locations. For this example our sample home was built after 1990, three-car attached garage, vaulted ceilings, unfinished basement, no crawlspace, no passive radon pipe, basement roughly 1400sq/ft in size with 3/4 inch gravel under the concrete slab.

A. Our first location option is adjacent to a sump pit near the front of the house. Sump pits are usually attached to an interior or exterior drainage system. This drain system can be used in place of a suction pit and can be very successful at mitigating radon. Placing an exterior system toward the front of the home is usually not our preferred option, but sometimes we already may have natural gas or other utilities in this location. Homeowners will generally plant bushes or flowers around these areas often concealing a well-designed system.

B. This is an excellent location due to its proximity to the furnace and water heater. The air conditioner unit would also be located in this area. If this basement were finished, the interior part of the system would be in the mechanical room and easily accessible. From the front of the home, this system is difficult to see. The length of the exhaust pipe would be determined by proximity to windows.

C & D. These are our two rear options. Homeowners may choose these locations due to duct pipes preventing other options, upper-level bedroom location, or maybe it fits into their basement finish design. For these locations, I like to try to keep the fan a couple of feet off of the corner to reduce noise at the rear of the house. The exhaust vent pipe is not easily visible from the front of the house at either location.

E&F. For these examples, we look at how a single suction pit can be used for either an interior system through the garage (F) or an exterior system (E) similar to the other examples. I like this location because you can easily route your system into the garage for an interior system or hide an exterior system behind the garage where it is not visible from the front. With interior garage systems, the fan is located in the garage rafters, not on the outside of the home. This design greatly reduces fan noise which may be an issue if the system is close to a bedroom or other quiet area.

These examples will be applicable for most homes except for some older and larger custom homes. Crawlspaces add a different dimension to the location selection. If the home is completely over a level and accessible crawlspace, the homeowner has many options. If the crawlspace is only under a single room or addition, then options become more limited. The idea here is not for realtors to be designing radon systems but to be aware of popular location options. Hopefully understanding the basics will help real estate professionals be a little more aware of how areas are selected for installation.

Post Mitigation Testing

Testing the home after the installation of any SSD system follows the same closed home conditions as the first test. Follow-up tests should be started approximately twelve hours after completion and activation of the new system and last for at least a minimum of forty-eight hours. Properly installed mitigation systems will begin removing soil gas immediately after the fan is turned on as noted in earlier examples.

The twelve-hour maturation time allows for the interior levels to stabilize so the post-mitigation test best represents the new radon levels for that home. EPA recommends homeowners should retest their homes every two years and many homes are retested at time of sale even if a mitigation system has been installed in the past. When an older home upgrades a furnace, water heater, or other utility, this can result in changes to airflow and radon entry. Discuss the changes with a radon professional. This might be a good time to retest the home and check radon levels.

Chapter 6
Municipalities

During my career, I have worked in quite a few local municipalities spanning four states and the District of Columbia. The expansion and construction in all these areas has been staggering. As areas become more crowded, some people naturally move farther away from the cities and out into the suburbs. Moving into smaller municipalities can mean a significant decrease in building costs and permits, but it can also mean less of a concern about issues such as radon.

Families that are moving to these areas are generally looking for something more affordable with more space for family or hobbies. The trend is to give the occupants more space, and with more space comes a larger home footprint. This increase in footprint means that folks run a higher risk of being on a radon emitting source.

Average Square Feet of New U.S. Single-Family Homes 1973-2010

General Radon Rule:

The greater the square footage of the footprint of a home, the greater the probability it will be over enough source material to elevate radon levels above the EPA action level of 4.0pCi/l.

This rule holds true for most homes in the continental United States and many other areas around the world. Homes that are being remodeled with new additions being added are also at risk. I have mitigated several homes where it has been obvious that the source was coming from a newer addition to the home. It is also important to note that many of these additions are used for master bedroom suites or family rooms that get used often by occupants.

While many are following this general trend of a larger home footprint, in some communities builders are constructing smaller homes that help younger families afford new construction in a master-planned community. These homes are generally smaller in size but can offer a well-designed upper level, two-car garage, and a full unfinished basement. With these communities, it is important to remember two important points:

1. Even though each home has less square footage, these communities can have more homes per acre so the amount of *"footprint"* per acre may be

much more than a development with larger homes and larger lots.

2. Because the homes are smaller with fewer bedrooms, homeowners are simply adding bedrooms in the basement for extra space. Many times these bedrooms are occupied by children.

How can Municipalities help?

In the world of home building and renovations, municipalities dictate how and when things get done. Municipalities are the ones who discharge the building permits, inspect the property at multiple stages of construction and issue the final occupancy permit so new homeowners can move in. Radon guidelines differ from county to county and so many municipalities simply refer back to the state which may or may not even address radon issues. As we have discussed before, builders, mortgage companies, real estate agents, home buyers, and sellers are becoming more aware of radon. Below I have listed a couple of recommendations for promoting radon awareness among the public and those in closely related trades. Please review these recommendations and consider formulating a plan of action so that municipalities are providing information on radon before new construction or renovations begin.

Provide access to inexpensive test kits

Testing for radon sounds expensive to most homeowners and in many instances, it can be. A radon test with a continuous radon monitor can cost anywhere from $150 to $200 for a forty-eight hour test. Simple passive test kits can range from $20 to $50 or more depending on where the test kit was purchased. Testing companies will give discounts for bulk purchase of test kits. Small municipalities can discuss these options with state agencies to take advantage of these savings and pass it on to residents. Discounted test kits can be sold at libraries, senior centers, and especially locations where building permits are obtained.

Mitigation/Testing Education

The EPA has an excellent radon promotion kit. It highlights many great ideas for promoting radon awareness in the community. These activities not only get residents to test their homes but give people a reason to learn more about radon, radiation, and new developments in associated fields. In my opinion, all municipalities should have some kind of local radon awareness and education program in place.

https://epapsa.com/images/radon_outreach_kit.pdf

Among the many good recommendations in the outreach kit, there is one course of action I would like to highlight. On page 6, the last recommendation under section 2, Engage Community Leaders, there is a small paragraph about coordinating with local utilities. This is an area I feel is underutilized. For an outreach program that helps minimize errors in the field, one recommendation is to increase information very specific about radon mitigation systems and testing directly to homeowners. Every few months new information could be included with the monthly bill discussing radon. Review a couple different types of testing methods. Explain the importance of having a RMT (Radon Mitigation Technician) number on the system and what this number means. Homeowners will see this information and it will start discussions with neighbors and friends. Indoor air quality is an important factor for good health.

Radon Disclosure/Warnings

In Colorado, radon disclosure is required in real estate transactions. Most states have either a disclosure rule or a warning about radon. This means the topic of radon has been discussed, but action is not required. A warning statement or disclosure is an effective way to address radon issues at the time of sale but does not address radon before work has begun.

Permits and Fees

In the radon industry there are a varied amount of players. Some carry the proper certifications, follow standard procedures and those that don't. Radon mitigation system installation includes knowledge in radon, concrete, building techniques, carpentry, electrical, plumbing, HVAC, roofing and water drainage.

Some states have begun adding additional certification requirements and fees to radon systems. Other municipalities have required permits for electrical work to radon fans. For large commercial projects these costs are expected as radon mitigation is most likely only one of several other projects going on at the worksite. For residential radon projects the case is just the opposite.

Additional costs added onto the price of radon systems leads to a direct *decrease* in participation rates.

Most homes contain more than one occupant and pet. Negative health effects caused from radon and over exposure to soil gases increase health care costs and decrease quality of life. We are not just trying to avoid a seasonal cold, but possibly cancers and illnesses of different types.

Each builder addresses radon in a different manner as well. Some include radon-resistant features in building plans while others do not. The following page has a copy of the EPA Radon-Resistant New Construction (RRNC) checklist. This is an excellent example of a simple form that could accompany building permits for new homes. Something similar could be drafted for renovations as well. This would give builders the opportunity to integrate radon systems into new construction projects from the very beginning. The forms would also assist residential contractors by alerting homeowners of radon testing and prevention techniques before renovations or remodeling occurs.

Radon-Resistant New Construction

FEATURES CHECKLIST

This house was built with basic, proven radon-resistant construction techniques. Reducing radon levels lowers your risk of radon-induced lung cancer. To help protect you, our company has included a radon reduction system in your new home. The system includes the following recommended radon-resistant features:

- ☑ **Gravel:** Applied a layer of clean, coarse gravel below the foundation or used an alternative, such as a perforated pipe or a collection mat.

- ☑ **Plastic Sheeting or Vapor Retarder:** Placed heavy-duty plastic sheeting or a vapor retarder over the gravel to inhibit radon and other soil gases from entering the house.

- ☑ **A Vent Pipe:** Installed a vent pipe vertically from the gravel layer through the house's conditioned space and roof. This safely vents radon and other soil gases outside the house.

- ☑ **Sealing and Caulking:** Sealed all openings, cracks, and crevices in the concrete foundation and walls with polyurethane caulk to prevent radon and other soil gases from entering the home.

- ☑ **Junction Box:** Installed an electrical junction box (outlet) in the attic for use with a vent fan, should, after testing for radon, a more robust system be needed.

Please contact us should you have any questions regarding the above features.

Builder's Signature _____ Date_____

House address _____

The U.S. EPA and the Surgeon General recommend that all homes be tested for radon. Please visit [www.epa.gov/radon/rrnc/index.html] or contact your state's radon office for more information.

The RRNC checklist addresses the most important parts of the radon system with simple descriptions of relevant tasks. The form does not have an area for an RMT or certification number. Any and all personnel installing radon mitigation piping should be certified and

185

have a RMT number. On many occasions, extra work is necessary because workers did not know how to correctly install a passive radon system. These mistakes lead to extra costs for future residents and elevated indoor radon levels until the problem is addressed. Passive systems installed by unqualified persons can result in systems that are dangerous for activation. I have personally seen this in new homes in my area. In chapter 7, there is a section that reviews the features of the RRNC checklist and explains each area in a little more detail.

The Realities of Radon

Over my career, I have installed radon systems for individuals in many different types of industries. One customer, in particular, is an inspector for a local municipality. At the time he was renovating a home previously owned by his father-in-law. They did a radon test soon after purchasing the home and wanted to add a radon system before finishing the basement. Luckily we had some time to chat, and so I asked him a few questions about the job and doing inspections for residential new construction. He told me about some of the frustrations with the job and we joked about topics neither of us had any control over. It was a fun conversation, and I am glad to have the opportunity to hear his perspective.

Years ago, my brother worked with a large firm placing commercial and residential tradesmen in different jobs across his local area. We would talk about the difficulties of finding qualified people, keeping employees working regularly, and some of the bizarre accidents that have happened at worksites. Issues that he was seeing on the job in Virginia are very similar to things that the Colorado inspector was commenting about as well. Builders and associated personnel sometimes make mistakes or overlook small details. Without a specific plan for radon, these mistakes are inevitable.

Reflecting on those conversations, it seems that expecting municipal home inspectors to be able to fully inspect each radon system is unreasonable. Radon planning should begin with the initial home blue prints not something that is designed during construction. I believe the effort would be better spent providing builders and associated contractors with the proper tools to make passive radon systems as efficient as possible. Including this type of radon information at the permitting stage will help contractors promote effective radon reduction techniques in residential projects. Constructing efficient passive radon systems allows for the effective use of energy-efficient fans if activation is necessary.

Chapter 7

New Construction/Contractors

Residential builders and contractors are placed in the arduous position of having to sift through all sorts of local and federal codes as well as look after the customers' demands and expectations. Many times, radon issues are addressed after a home has already been built, or the basement finish has been started. This can lead to radon pipes being placed in finished interior spaces or exhaust vent pipes placed in unattractive exterior locations. By being proactive when it comes to radon issues, customers can enjoy a more efficient, consumer-friendly system that will lead to increased value for the home and a better state of mind for the people living in that property.

Why Is This Important To Customers?

For most of us, our home is the single largest investment we will ever make. Basement finishes or remodeling can cost tens of thousands of dollars and involve countless hours spent in planning and preparation. The majority of homeowners are unfamiliar with their own homes, attics, crawlspaces, and sump pits. Until they become more actively involved, they will not see the potential for the intrusion of soil gas, mold, and mildew growth. These areas are attractive place for insects to live and breed as well. Most folks will agree that these are not activities they want occurring in their homes.

Another important feature of radon systems is moisture removal. There are prevention methods but the reality is that water will find a way underneath the basement slab eventually. Excessive moisture can lead to concrete cracking and upheaval even when a sump pit and piping has been installed. Sub-floor piping is directed to the sump pit for discharge but the pipes are not always sloped properly to provide flawless drainage. Concrete upheaval can be extremely expensive and frustrating for homeowners using ridged floor finishes such as tile or other flooring products. I have seen this happen in many new home basements around my area.

The last and most important reason to incorporate radon prevention techniques into every home is health. A home will change hands many times. Each family will have several members and pets. The probability of radon or excessive soil gas doing damage increases with time, exposure, home use, and number of occupants. Only the goldfish is safe from radon. A well-designed and installed radon system helps efficiently decrease contaminants entering the breathable airspace for improved health over the lifetime of the home for all occupants.

RRNC in Depth

When it comes to new homes, the builders have the opportunity to design and install highly efficient, passive radon systems. Unfortunately, radon systems are often not designed or installed by qualified professionals. Building a quality passive radon system begins before the basement floor is poured, and ends almost at time of occupancy. Multiple trades work on a radon system throughout the process. It is easy for mistakes to happen without proper communication and a formulated plan. By integrating passive radon mitigation into the original home designs, builders can help provide a superior product that will last a lifetime.

Radon-Resistant New Construction

FEATURES CHECKLIST

This house was built with basic, proven radon-resistant construction techniques. Reducing radon levels lowers your risk of radon-induced lung cancer. To help protect you, our company has included a radon reduction system in your new home. The system includes the following recommended radon-resistant features:

- ☑ **Gravel:** Applied a layer of clean, coarse gravel below the foundation or used an alternative, such as a perforated pipe or a collection mat.

- ☑ **Plastic Sheeting or Vapor Retarder:** Placed heavy-duty plastic sheeting or a vapor retarder over the gravel to inhibit radon and other soil gases from entering the house.

- ☑ **A Vent Pipe:** Installed a vent pipe vertically from the gravel layer through the house's conditioned space and roof. This safely vents radon and other soil gases outside the house.

- ☑ **Sealing and Caulking:** Sealed all openings, cracks, and crevices in the concrete foundation and walls with polyurethane caulk to prevent radon and other soil gases from entering the home.

- ☑ **Junction Box:** Installed an electrical junction box (outlet) in the attic for use with a vent fan, should, after testing for radon, a more robust system be needed.

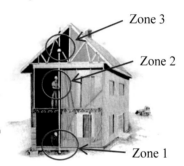

Zone 3

Zone 2

Zone 1

Please contact us should you have any questions regarding the above features.

Builder's Signature _____ Date_____

House address _____

The U.S. EPA and the Surgeon General recommend that all homes be tested for radon. Please visit [www.epa.gov/radon/rrnc/index.html] or contact your state's radon office for more information.

Above is a copy of the EPA's RRNC checklist. The pictured home has been allocated into Zones 1-3. Let us look at each zone and explain in a little more detail the importance of each feature of the checklist.

Zone 1

Zone 1 is the most important part of the system. Preparation underneath the basement slab is directly proportional to passive system radon removal rates. The idea is to allow room under the slab so gas can easily flow into the pipes and out the exhaust.

Gravel: The checklist recommends coarse gravel or an alternative product under the basement slab. This is fine if you are going to activate the system with a fan, but it is not the best approach if you are designing a quality passive radon system. The best way to allow the soil gas to flow is to use clean 5/8" to 1 ½" gravel approximately 4" deep and a 3" perforated collection pipe under the slab. On the following page is a chart of gravel size vs. porosity.

The larger size gravel is really the best option under the basement slab. Pea gravel works well with a good pipe design, but when the footprint size goes up, a passive system can become less effective. Smaller gravel sizes can either have good porosity due to uneven settling under the home, or poor porosity as they mix with finer material or undergo compaction. Sandy and high silt-clay soils can become very tight especially with the addition of moisture, minimizing communication underneath the basement slab.

Size vs Porosity	
Gravel 5/8"- 1 1/2" clean	**Excellent**
Pea Gravel ¼"- 5/8" clean	**Good**
0.2" – 7/16"	**Fair-Poor**
Sandy Soils	**Poor**
High silt-clay content soil	**Very poor**

Plastic Sheet or Vapor Retarder: A plastic vapor barrier beneath the basement slab offers an additional layer of separation between soil gas and interior space. This contributes to the efficiency of the passive system and helps minimize losses due to concrete settling and cracking.

Sealing and Chalking: A passive radon mitigation system will not work to the best of its abilities if the basement is not sealed properly. Sump pits, bathroom rough-ins, expansion joints, perimeter gaps, utility pipes, and any other floor penetrations will all need to be addressed during this process. Construction dirt does have the potential to contain radon source material. Remove dirt and debris from the basement to provide a better surface for chalk and sealants as well as minimize any potential source material. If a furnace is to be placed close to an exterior wall, make sure to ask that the adjacent wall be sealed before installation. The objective of these efforts is to stop the soil gas from entering the home and help it enter the pipe system so it can discharge outside.

Sub-Slab Pipe Design

Here are a few basic sub-slab pipe designs. Let's do a quick review of the designs.

Design 1

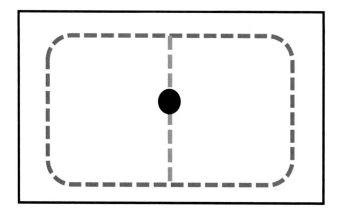

Design 1: This typical layout would be to run a three or four-inch perforated interior perimeter drain pipe, roughly eighteen inches from your footers to a centralized vertical stem. This is quite similar to a sump pit system. The design works well for a passive system and even better when activated.

Design 2

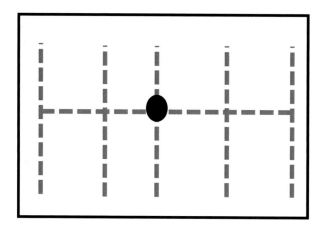

Design 2: Here we have multiple pathways available to a central stem in a H pattern. This design works very well with tighter backfill material but will be more expensive due to extra pipe and fittings. The extra pipe increases probability of being close to source material so that radon can easily enter the system and exhaust outside.

Design 3

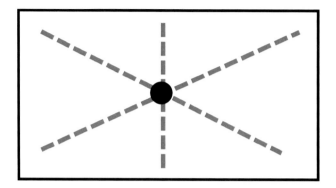

Design 3: Here is my first recommendation for the most effective passive radon system. The pipe creates multiple direct pathways for the gas to travel to the central stem. The objective is to minimize the distance from the source, to the collection pipe.

This design, like the other examples, should be altered to fit your unique project and obstacles. A specific pattern is not as important as understanding the basic principles and putting some effort and thought into sub-slab pipe design and installation. Residential contractors and concrete personnel should understand the importance of these pipes. Each home will have some levels of radon and many will be excessively elevated.

Zone 2

Vent Pipe: The RRNC checklist picture shows a wonderful example of a very efficient pipe run. Unfortunately, integrating passive radon systems into today's home designs can be challenging and rarely as straightforward as the example pictured. Several key concepts must be acknowledged for a passive radon system to work at its peak efficiency.

Straight, vertical runs work best!

Horizontal runs and ninety degree bends place resistance on airflow in the pipe. Use forty-five degree bends and minimize horizontal runs in order to promote better airflow. Moisture will build up inside the pipe, active or passive. Activated radon systems move a lot of moisture! Make sure fittings are glued and sloped properly to avoid possible water leaks.

Route the radon pipe through a central location to help take advantage of the stack effect!

In winter months, conditioned interior air warms the pipe promoting the flow of soil gas up the pipe and to the exhaust. In summer months the heat of an attic space can help promote the same movement of gas. Radon pipes should be in centralized locations and not inside exterior walls.

Pipe size: I always go with four inch pipe especially in homes with a basement area over 850sq/ft. If the sub-slab pipe is well designed in combination with gravel and vapor barrier, three inch pipe can be used for the vertical pipe with good passive system results. Placing system labels on the pipe is always recommended.

Zone 3

Junction Box: Attics and crawlspaces are confined spaces. Both should be fitted with at least one working light and/or an electrical outlet for power. The RRNC calls for an electrical junction box to activate the system if a fan is needed. The electrical outlet should be located roughly one to two feet from the pipe and ready for use. Builders can expect to see 10 - 35% (or greater) activation rates in many areas. All confined spaces in your home should be periodically inspected for damage, moisture or animal activity.

Here are a couple extra details not included in the Zone 3 section.

Pipe Clearance: Pipe should have a vertical clearance with a minimum of three to four feet above attic insulation and six to eight inches on either side of the pipe in case system activation is necessary. Radon pipes should be accessible!! The more complex the attic, the greater the need for radon pipe planning. Radon pipes in locations far away from the attic entrance or hard to access areas make system activation dangerous for the technician. Safety should always be a consideration.

Varmint guard: Install a varmint guard at the end of the exhaust pipe to keep animals outside. This is something that is often overlooked in new construction. Air moving through the system can be much warmer than exterior air and enticing to rodents or birds. Varmint guards help keep critters out of the pipe so the passive system can do its job effectively.

There are many little details involved with installing a passive radon system. Radon is extremely small and the currents that make the system work are quite gentle. Each zone plays a specific role in the system. If the basic principles are not understood then items can get overlooked, which can easily reduce the system efficiency to zero.

Value of the System

After reviewing everything involved with a passive system, it is easy to see just how much planning is really needed. Even after you've done all this work, the home has still not been tested and may need activation to further decrease levels. I don't know of any other trade that requires so much attention from start to finish.

Passive systems can help remove some sub-slab moisture but in most cases a fan is needed. Activating a well-designed passive system will remove moisture and reduce radon at the same time. The best part is that manufacturers are producing low-wattage, energy-efficient fans. These fans cost less to purchase and less to operate. The key to using low-flow fans is having well-designed sub-slab pipes and gravel underneath the basement floor. Skipping key steps, especially in Zone 1, can greatly reduce efficiency and make the energy-efficient fans completely ineffective.

From my experience, it seems like most builders are irritated by having to install passive radon systems in new homes. Regardless of the benefits, radon systems often seem to be carelessly installed. Site managers cannot afford to spend time on all the various details for free. For these reasons, I ask builders to consider the following recommendations and follow through with a plan that works for their organization.

1. ***Charge the right amount of money needed for the system to be completed properly.*** Passive radon systems are not free. They take time, thought, and effort to be installed correctly. Customers are willing to pay for a quality product that is well designed and efficient. Corrections to radon systems after home completion can be difficult, expensive, and embarrassing to the builder.

2. *Design a unique radon system for each model of home offered.*

One size does not fit all. Work with a local radon firm to ensure that designs meet all relevant building codes and help minimize mistakes. Good designs are energy friendly over the life of the home. In most cases, a radon firm will not be doing the installation. Have instructions prepared on each zone for contractors to follow. Include contingency plans for additions, crawlspaces or other options that may be available.

3. *Recommend a few local companies for activation and testing.*

If a builder installs a well-designed passive system, they are mitigating part of the soil gas as a result of the design. The step in the process should be transferred to radon professionals. They can help best explain radon test results and indoor air quality issues. System activations, fan replacements, testing, manometers, alarms, and inspections should all be handled by a firm specific to radon. Customers will need radon specific services in the future. I don't think builders want to be servicing calls about loud fans or broken manometers.

Finishing the Basement / Additions

A homeowner's decision to finish their basement or add an addition to the home is usually driven by any one of many motivating factors. Whatever the case may be, the end result is that the new finished space will see a lot of activity from the occupants once complete. A home addition will add to the square footage of the home but more importantly from a radon perspective, increase the home footprint and probability for elevated levels. This is an excellent reason to discuss testing and the possible installation of a radon system. It is important for homeowners to understand that by taking preventive measures before construction begins, they will help increase the system's performance and add value through efficient design. Here are the three basics you need to implement before the framing goes up for that basement expansion.

1. **Test the basement**: This should always be the first step, especially if no previous tests have been conducted. If a test was done more than two to three years ago, it might be a good idea to retest the home. Chapter 2 goes over a lot of the testing basics. Call a local professional if you have more questions about testing in your area.

2. **Review the design**: In Chapter 5, there is a section that goes over the basics of radon system placement. There may already be a utility area or closet that would work well if a system is needed. The more area that is finished, the more difficult it can be to find an acceptable location for a radon system. Being proactive at this stage is always recommended.

3. **Seal and Caulk**: This should be first before framing goes up for any basement finish. Pay special attention to basement corners and utility pipes as discussed earlier. Sump pits should have a cover that can be sealed down, preferably with a viewport to observe any future water accumulation. Use expansion foam for areas under bathtubs and any other floor penetrations as needed.

Additions: With home additions there is no way to know if the new area will increase radon levels prior to completion so it is simply best to plan it in. Discuss any home tests that may have been performed or connecting onto an existing system if that is an option. If the addition is over a crawlspace, plan to cover and seal the exposed soil and any other entry points. Remove crawlspace debris and provide a relatively flat surface for the vapor barrier. Install a soil gas collection pipe and riser especially if the home has never been tested. Customers may want an active system in a crawlspace area for moisture, mildew and dust reduction.

Minimize Your Risk

When working in the trades, it can be easy to ignore personal safety to get the job done quickly. I have unfortunately made this mistake more than a few times. Here I would like to make a few recommendations for contractors to help reduce exposure to radon, VOCs and fine particulates/dust.

- Air out the Space - Open things up and try to create a cross current for a few minutes to evacuate airborne contaminants before work begins. Fine particles and gas do not take long to move from the space when given the opportunity. Radon can build up over the evening hours. Radon daughters can attach to fine airborne particles due to construction activities and can be inhaled if not ventilated.

- Know your Products – Review the MDS sheets for job products used. Unfortunately, the same products that help us do our jobs do produce airborne contaminants such as VOC's. This includes things like paint, caulking, carpets, and adhesives. Be aware of the type and quantity of products used.

- Mask Up - Working in confined spaces such as crawlspaces and attics can stir up very fine particles that go unnoticed and easily enter the breathable air space. Our chart in Chapter 2 lists household dust as small as 0.05 microns! Drilling holes through concrete and wood creates lots of fine particles. Half-face masks are very effective at removing most of these contaminants and are economical to purchase. I like to completely replace my half-face mask about every 3-4 months and clean it thoroughly after dirty jobs. It is worth every penny.

Chapter 8

Health and Final Thoughts

" I am among those who think that science has

great beauty. A scientist in his laboratory is not only a

technician: he is also a child placed before natural

phenomena which impress him like a fairy tale."

- Madam Marie Curie

Advances in technology and theory have opened up amazing new areas of opportunity and knowledge. This section on health will focus in part on understanding how radiation and radon pollution can affect the body. It will also look at a statement about Personalized Risk in radiology. Finally, all this will be tied together in the Final Thoughts section. For many of us, it is difficult to understand that radon, an invisible gas, is a radioactive form of air pollution. The radon gas itself is not so much the problem as its decay cycle and daughters thereafter. In chapter two there was a brief description of the radon daughters and possible side effects from overexposure. The real mystery is all about the radiation. How dangerous is this stuff and what can it do to people?

While doing some basic internet research, I stumbled upon a question asked on quora.com. The question was: Why is nuclear radiation more dangerous than other forms of pollution? Sometimes responses on these websites are rather silly, but more often than not, the answers posted are submitted by informed and knowledgeable people. I have selections from two answers I would like to focus on. The first answer was provided by Robert Gauthier of Montreal, Canada, and the second is from David McFarland, US Navy.

Question: *Why is nuclear radiation more dangerous than other forms of pollution?*

Answered Dec 6, 2017, Robert Gauthier, Montreal Canada

"It isn't. As with everything, the dose makes the poison: low levels of ionizing radiation are less harmful than high levels of other toxins. However, humanity has been living with chemical and biological hazards for a very long time, and because these are familiar, most believe that they can evaluate the risk. Radiation, on the other hand, is perceived as something novel and is largely misunderstood. It is invisible, and you cannot feel it, taste it, or smell it, and this gives it an aura of something insidious that cannot be avoided."

I chose this statement because of the focus on dose and perception. Most of us do not understand the concept of radiation dose. Our perception of radiation is mostly associated with words like contamination, waste, and cancer. He also refers to other chemical and biological hazards in the environment. Identifying and minimizing exposure to any of these hazards should always be the goal.

Next, let us read a selection taken from the answer provided by Mr. McFarland.

Answered Feb 14, 2018, David McFarland, Reactor Operator at United States Navy

"Get enough of the stuff - or just the right singular bit of radiation that happens to irradiate the right cell, without the body's defenses catching on as they usually do - and you can get cancer.

The radiation emitted by radioactive elements can strike the cell in one of two ways:

- Direct DNA damage.

- Ionizing water/radiolytic decomposition of water, causing chemical chain-reactions, which then could damage DNA if it's in the right part of the cell.

Most of the time, even when your DNA is damaged, the cell repairs it. On rare occasion, it destroys a *"spare"* telomere. But as you age, your cells slowly lose these, and copying of DNA isn't always perfect. Sometimes your body makes a mistake, or radiation damages the DNA, making an improper write-over.

Often times, this has little to no effect.

Sometimes the cell sees the damage and kills itself. If this does not occur, usually other cells trigger its own death - and if not this, then white-blood cells do.

Usually, the cell dies, one way or another, or it survives but its cell-daughters are not viable and die.

But, not always. Sometimes the damaged cell becomes cancer - it grows uncontrollably, not performing its usual functions, hurting the body."

Mr. McFarland's answer gets straight to the point by addressing the two different ways cells can be damaged, directly or indirectly. To explain this in a little more detail, I needed to borrow some notes from the Coursera class: Life, Health, and Radiation by University of Sydney.

Class notes:

There are direct and indirect ways the cells in our body are affected by ionization. If radiation ionizes atoms in DNA molecules or some other parts of the cell that are critical to its survival, then we say it has had a direct effect. The creation of ions can physically break either the sugar-phosphate backbone of the DNA or its base pairs. Sometimes this damage can affect the ability of the cell to reproduce and ultimately survive. It's actually quite unlikely that radiation would interact directly with DNA molecules, as they occupy only a tiny fraction of the cell. As you know, atoms are mostly empty, and the radiation passes right through them.

Indirect effects of radiation are much more common, as most of the cell volume is water. There is a much higher probability that the radiation interacts with this water in a process called radiolysis. What is radiolysis? Basically, the radiation breaks the bonds holding water molecules together and produces hydrogen and hydroxyl radicals. If oxygen is also present, then other more aggressive free radicals form as well, such as hydroperoxyl and hydrogen peroxide. Free radicals are uncharged molecules which have an unpaired valence electron in their outer shell. This makes them highly chemically reactive. In other words, they'd very easily bond to other atoms and molecules. This means that they damage the cell by causing structural changes to the DNA or other parts of the cell.

For example, free radicals such as hydroxyl can

remove hydrogens that are bonded to carbons in the deoxyribose sugar backbone of the DNA. This starts off a chain reaction which eventually results in a strand break. Some free radicals are able to remove hydrogens from both strands of the DNA, which eventually produces a double-strand break. If not repaired, then it may result in apoptosis or self-destruction of the cell.

When ionizing radiation damages the DNA, there are essentially four possible outcomes. One outcome is that the damage may be repaired and the cell survives. Another possible outcome is that the damaged DNA cannot be repaired, and this, unfortunately, leads to the death of the cell. It is also possible for the damage to affect the reproduction of the cell. So the daughter cells die. (Daughter cells are those cells that result from the division of a cell when it reproduces itself.) Lastly, the damage may not be repaired at all. But a mutation occurs, and the cell survives to pass on its damaged DNA. If enough mutated cells survive, they can undergo rapid cell division and form a new growth called a neoplasm, also called a tumor. Sometimes these neoplasms can be benign, so unharmful to our health. But other times these tumors can be malignant, or what we call cancerous.

There is one other section from class that I wanted to pay special attention to. This next section is on personalized risk. It is important to note that the Human Genome Project currently estimates that each human has somewhere between 20,000 to 25,000 genes!

Personalized Risk

Since the publication of the Human Genome Project in 2001, genome sequencing technologies have revealed that there are individuals in the population that have situations or single nucleotide polymorphisms which render them unable to repair the DNA properly. In fact, variations in radiosensitivity have been recognized for over 100 years. According to the recent Next Generation Sequencing projects, between 8.5-17 percent of particular cancer patients have germline that is inherited mutations in their DNA damage response pathways. This goes a long way toward explaining why they develop cancer, but should also inform us of how we approach these individuals with respect to ionizing radiation exposure.

As modern medicine pushes toward a more individualized or precision approach, it stands to reason that we can use this DNA sequencing data to tailor our imaging approaches. For example,

have you heard of the so-called *"breast cancer genes?"* Well, actually, we all have these genes! But what the media is usually referring to are mutations in two very famous breast cancer-associated genes, BRCA1 and BRCA2. These mutations alter the functions of the BRCA1 and BRCA2 proteins encoded within these genes so that they don't work properly anymore. BRCA1 and BRCA2 proteins are part of the DNA damage response of the cell.

So people who inherited these mutations are less likely to be able to repair damage to their DNA and are thus likelier to develop cancer in their lifetime, than people with working BRCA1 and BRCA2. With respect to ionizing radiation, these individuals may be as much as fifty times more sensitive to radiation than the general population. That's fifty times less likely to repair the damage. In fact, women who carry mutations in these genes, and who were exposed to mammograms before the age of thirty, were found to have a higher incidence of cancer than those who were not. It may not be too long before the radiology information systems we use in the clinic incorporate some form of indicator that steers these patients away from ionizing modalities in favor of non-ionizing alternatives, such as clinical examination, ultrasound, or MRI.

Until then, it's best to assume that anyone could be a carrier of BRCA1 and two mutations. Therefore, we observe the ALARA principle. A safety principle to minimize radiation doses by employing all reasonable methods. To conclude, whilst current guidelines are simple to understand and implement, they fail to acknowledge recent developments in our understanding of radio-biology and the variation that exists within the human population. As this understanding develops, it stands to reason that our models will become increasingly sophisticated, and even tailored toward the individual.

The thought that effects from ionizing radiation can be passed down from generation to generation is frightening and fascinating. It may also help to shed some light on how and why cancer develops in younger patients. This really seems to be an amazing time to be involved in radiological fields of study.

Final Thoughts

For most of us, we equate radon with lung cancer and smoking. Sometimes you don't have to smoke to get lung cancer. Radon, a gas, is ionizing radiation which is in a constant state of decay. It is in our air space, and we breathe it in. If the amount is too high, it decays in our lungs, causing lung cancer. Correct? The answer is yes for some, no for others, and a maybe for your children. Very confusing.

Just like the radon levels in your home, your personal risk is individualistic. The risk for you, your spouse, family, and the pets is unique. Young people are at risk because they have time to develop cancers. Older people are at risk because their ability to fight off cancers has decreased. Middle-aged people are at risk because cancer may have already developed within their bodies, or continued exposure could trigger some recessive cancer. Pets are at risk because they are closer to the source, have higher respiration rates, and love to play in the dirt.

Earlier, we spent some time discussing dose and radiation. In chapter 3, I present several homes with extreme indoor radon fluctuations. We look at how the radon increases well above the reported averages for just a few hours a day now and again. Day after day the radon levels fluctuate, increasing dose whenever conditions are right. A few of my examples occurred during extreme summertime weather events with the exception of my house. My home was just under normal winter conditions for a February. The point being is that during these times of poor weather we are typically in the home and possibly using the lower levels, thus increasing exposure to you and your family. This does not happen in just a few homes, it is a common occurrence in many, many homes.

In chapter 2, we look at the size of radon in comparison to things we can see. Radon and radon daughters are very, very small. Objects of this size act in ways that are all their own and the damage they do is unique. The reality is that many homes have been exposing the occupants to excessive doses of radon possibly over multiple generations. This exposure may bear partial responsibility for some of the cancers or inherited mutations we see today.

Earlier, we looked at an online answer posted by Mr. Gauthier referring to pollution and dose.

"As with everything, the dose makes the poison: low levels of ionizing radiation are less harmful than high levels of other toxins."

Toxic chemicals are everywhere, and more are being created each year. Almost every industry uses a large amount of chemicals and there is no way to get around it. Unfortunately not only are these chemicals abundant in our workplaces but in our homes as well. Something as simple as painting the interior of our homes or getting new carpets. Without proper ventilation we are inadvertently exposing ourselves to an excessive dose of contaminants. An occasional incident is not much of a concern in most cases, but my thoughts are about the constant exposure that is just below our detection levels. What happens when radon is introduced into the equation? We may not be able to avoid contaminants altogether, but we can take action to reduce some exposure.

It is difficult to think about our homes as active, *"living"* systems, but that is what we create for ourselves. The inside of the home has many parts of circulation. The outside of the home is subjected to constant stress from wind, humidity, gravity, precipitation, temperature, and atmospheric pressure. Design and building materials also affect interior air dynamics. Underneath the home there are chemical reactions, earth gases and constant movement of the strata. All ultimately negatively affecting the indoor air quality in your home.

Removing radon from your home is just one small way to improve the health of you and your family. The effects of radon and soil gas exposure have been noted for hundreds of years. After Marie Curie discovered radium and its properties, businesses came out with many different products for its use well before it was truly understood. Many wonderful advances in medicine did occur at that time but products for public consumption and industry killed hundreds if not thousands of people as well. Today we know more about the dangers of radium and radon, but our knowledge is still limited.

Radon is now mostly associated with smoking and lung cancer. Ionizing radiation and the daughters produced from radon do not discriminate. Because it is a gas most of us assume there is a direct cause/effect relationship to lung cancer. A strong relationship to lung cancer does exist, but we must not rule out radon's possible role in other forms of cancer or genetic mutations. Developments in the study of lung cancer have been moving at a very fast pace.

I recently stumbled upon the following article that looks at how lung cancer can move to other areas of the body:

https://www.everydayhealth.com/lung-cancer/living-with/how-lung-cancer-progresses-stage/

Just like we discussed earlier, it seems cancer can start in the lungs then move to other parts of the body. Cancers such as brain, bone, adrenal gland, liver, pancreas, stomach, small and large intestine, skin, eyes, kidneys, and breast could all be assisted by elevated levels of radon in the breathable airspace. Hopefully, new studies can help to add clarity in this area. I would like to see much more research related to radon and cancer.

Radium decays from a solid to a gas. Radon!

Then... back to a solid.

Simply Amazing!!